Seduction of the Heart

Seduction of the Heart

How to Guard and Keep
Your Heart from Evil

TIM LaHAYE
AND
ED HINDSON

W PUBLISHING GROUP™
www.wpublishinggroup.com

A Division of Thomas Nelson, Inc.
www.ThomasNelson.com

ISBN 0-8499-1726-3

Printed in the United States of America
2 3 4 BVG 9 8 7 6 5 4 3 2 1

Contents

Part Two · HEART FAILURE

Part Three · HEART TO HEART

Part Four · A HEART LIKE HIS

Preface

OUR EMOTIONS CAN CAUSE US SERIOUS PROBLEMS. Emotions can confuse our thinking, disturb our hearts, sap our vitality, and disrupt our walks with God. Anger, guilt, fear, and worry take an incredible toll on our well-being. In fact, doctors tell us that nearly 70 percent of all illnesses are emotionally induced.

Most of us are stretched beyond our limits. We give of ourselves mentally, emotionally, and spiritually, pouring our hearts and souls into our jobs and families. But we do very little to guard our hearts and replenish our fast-paced lives.

Disappointment and unfulfilled expectations are the results. Our marriages are failing, our children are hurting, and our lives are coming apart. It is time to stop and ask ourselves what is really important in life. Our hearts would say that peace, contentment, and personal satisfaction are more important than the meaningless pursuit of material gratification. We should listen.

This book will speak to your heart about the really important issues of life. It will challenge your thinking, examine your culture, and call you back to what really matters. It is a message of hope for people who have lost hope, for those who are searching for something deeper in their lives. Most of all, this book points to the timeless truths of God that can make a difference for us all.

The Meeting:
A Short Story

TEARS WERE PART OF THE MEETING.

It had been that way since the beginning. But always they belonged to other people. The faceless tide of troubled folk who washed up on the shores of Micah Phillips's crisis intervention meeting every Wednesday, any season of the year. Battered women, guilty men, depressed souls, lonely octogenarians.

All struggling for answers and a reason to live.

Micah swallowed hard and forced the day's events into the recesses of her mind. Then she mentally put on her-counselor hat and took her spot amid the five people who had come to her that day searching for answers.

"I'm Micah Phillips." Her gaze made its way around the small circle, locking eyes with each person. "Welcome to Heart Crisis Intervention."

She explained that after the two-hour meeting an evaluation would be made. Typically participants would be placed into an appropriate weekly outpatient group. Other times a recommendation would be made for hospitalization.

"We'll start with revelation. Each of you can talk about what brought you here . . . share your story. We'll have a question-answer session after that, and end with group closure."

The faces in the circle hung on every word, and Micah felt her confidence grow. She knew the basic details of their stories. It was part of the job, familiarizing herself with a group before actually meeting them. She prided herself on being their beacon of light, their source of hope. It was her place to sit above them and hand out advice.

But today the truth was something entirely different, and she hoped with every breath that the ocean of tears welling in her heart would not break free.

At least until she got home.

Because today, regardless of the stories she was about to hear, she had done something she never planned on doing.

She had become one of them.

"All right . . ." She sat a bit straighter. "Who would like to go first?"

Mark Adams was neither nervous nor fearful of the opportunity to tell his story. After more than a year of keeping silent about his darkest secrets, he was practically bursting to share them with the group. In some ways the things he was about to say were no different than a tragic closing argument or a dissertation on behalf of a doomed client.

A client with blood on his hands.

The difference was that these were not someone else's sordid details designed to sway a jury.

They were his own.

"Hi." He looked around the room and saw trembling hands on three of his peers. He was an attorney, trained to notice such things. He inhaled deeply. "I heard about Micah's program on the radio and decided to come. No one forced me." He rubbed his hands together. "I'm having panic attacks and . . ." His voice broke and his cheeks grew hot. He had promised himself not to get emotional. Certainly he was professional enough to keep his feelings at bay for one brief discussion.

He cleared his throat and continued. "My wife moved out six weeks ago, and, well . . . I feel like a murderer." He glanced at his shoes, unable to make eye contact through his tears. "It's a long story."

Micah shifted her position. "We have time. Why don't you start at the beginning?"

Mark nodded and allowed himself to drift back to that sunny autumn day more than a year ago. The day his young partner Leslie Landers first brought her personal feelings into his office.

Until that time, everything about Mark Adams's life had been measured and planned. He'd earned the right grades and attended the right schools. He passed the bar exam on the first try and avoided the type of serious relationship that might derail his career.

"I'll marry when I'm thirty-six," he liked to say. "Kids will come a few years later."

After a decade of climbing the corporate legal ladder, he met Susan on a Caribbean cruise and fell in love. They married three weeks after Mark's thirty-sixth birthday and had three children by the time they celebrated their sixth anniversary.

Just like Mark had planned.

"I always believed I'd be faithful to Susan." He sucked in a slow breath through clenched teeth. "But that was before I got to know Leslie. She was young and beautiful with a convincing manner and a mind like a steel trap. We were friendly with each other, of course, but I kept my distance. There was enough attraction between us for me to know better."

The story spilled from his heart, and in no time he forgot about the strangers seated around him. All that remained was the sad, sorry tale of Mark Adams's life, every dark and devastating detail.

It started in the fall after Leslie's live-in boyfriend moved out. They'd planned to marry within the year, and after the breakup she seemed always on the verge of tears. One morning Mark was in the break room stirring vanilla syrup into his coffee when Leslie walked in, took a seat, and quietly began to cry.

"I remember something warning me to be polite, to ask her if she was okay, then leave it alone." Mark shrugged. "But that wasn't what came out."

Instead he sat across from her and gently took her hands in his. "I know things have been hard at home." He spoke quietly. "My office door is open. If you need a friend, you've got one."

He remembered her reaction. She looked intently at him, the hint of a smile playing on her lips. "I might take you up on that."

Though the sadness remained, there was something deep and dangerous about the depth of gratitude in her eyes. When Mark walked away, his heart was beating strangely, pounding and skittering about, searching for a way back to normalcy. *She won't come*, he told himself. *I was just being polite.*

But at five o'clock that evening she proved him wrong. Most of the staff was gone when she knocked at the door and let herself in. "Have a minute?"

Even now he remembered the way his breath caught in his throat as he looked up from a legal docket and saw her there. She was achingly lovely, and in a matter of seconds he mentally postponed the dinner date he had with Susan, his wife. "Sure." He pointed to a chair on the other side of his desk. "Have a seat."

He closed the docket and cocked his head, trying everything in his power to dispel his building attraction to her. "What's up?"

She folded her hands in her lap and told him about her broken relationship. "He thought I was too busy for him." Tears welled in her eyes. "I never thought my schedule would come between us, never in a million years."

"I understand." Mark felt a connection growing between them, a garden of common ground. "A lawyer's schedule can be brutal on relationships."

Leslie wiped a tear from her cheek. "How do you do it? You and your wife seem so happy."

Mark considered his marriage and knew it wasn't true. He and Susan had troubles like anyone else—especially when it came to his schedule. He chuckled softly and admitted something he hadn't shared with anyone. "We're good at pretending."

THE MEETING: A SHORT STORY

They spent the next hour discussing the pitfalls of legal work and the inability to find anyone who might understand. Mark shared things about Susan that he'd only mildly considered in the past. But hearing them verbalized gave them a layer of truth and made his marriage—which had only hours earlier seemed fairly good—feel like little more than a sham.

He and Leslie talked about the cases they were working on, and in the process Mark found himself laughing at the same times she laughed, sharing similar values and insights and understandings. It was 6:30 and dark outside when Mark finally looked at his watch and grimaced. Susan had been looking forward to dinner on the town. Now he'd have to call and make up an excuse, tell her he'd gotten caught up in a last-minute case. "I have to get home."

Leslie was quiet a moment. "I know." A shadow of loneliness fell across her face.

Mark had the sudden unexplainable urge to ask her out, share the evening with her, and find a way to make her smile again. Susan would understand. After all, business meetings were part of the job.

He pictured his wife sitting home waiting for him, and he silently chastised himself. No, dinner with Leslie would not be a good idea. Not tonight. Instead he smiled and lowered his voice. "This was nice." He reached across his desk and as he'd done in the break room earlier, he squeezed her

7

hand. "It's been a long time since I've talked like that with anyone." He hesitated and felt his guard slipping. "Especially someone . . . as beautiful as you."

Leslie blushed, and something in the way she lingered in his office making small talk for another half-hour told him she was equally attracted. That night on the way home, Mark pondered the office conversation. It was a good thing, really. Mark was forty-six and Leslie, twenty-five. There couldn't possibly be anything romantic between them. They were coworkers, after all. Things were bound to be smoother, more efficient, if he and Leslie were connected at a deeper level.

Mark paused and felt the memory of those days fade.

He worked the muscles in his jaw and met the eyes of those in the circle. "When I got home, Susan had been crying. I knew we had dinner plans, but I'd completely forgotten why. It was her birthday. It took weeks before things felt normal between us."

He drifted back once more and remembered out loud how the meeting with Leslie led to others. Three months later they were sharing lunches and meeting in his office at least once a week.

"I could feel the attraction between us growing." Mark narrowed his eyes, wishing for a way to go back and do things differently. "I had no idea how serious things would get."

Their evening talks grew longer and more personal, and Mark felt himself falling in love with her. But he convinced himself the feeling wasn't mutual. She might have found him attractive, but he was old enough to be her father.

The changes happened gradually. Mark noticed differences in the way Leslie treated him in front of others. They'd be in a group meeting and his eyes would meet hers. Whereas in the past she might have smiled politely or nodded her head, now she would blush, her gaze falling to her hands.

Often when he was at the copier, she would brush up against him and whisper, "I need to talk to you . . . wait for me tonight, okay?"

Even the slightest feel of her skin against his ignited a fire that built with each passing day.

One evening he was working late when she walked into his office unannounced, closed the door, and locked it. Before he could find his voice, she came around his desk and pulled him to his feet. Her voice was nervous, vulnerable. "Hold me, Mark. Just hold me. I need a hug."

Think of Susan, he told himself. But before the thoughts were fully formed, his arms came around Leslie's waist and he pulled her close, his body fitting snugly against hers. He could feel her chest shaking and he realized she was crying. He leaned back enough to see her face. "What is it? What's wrong?"

She blinked back the tears and searched his face. "I'm . . . I'm in love with you, Mark. There's no other way to say it."

Mark remembered even now the way his world tilted wildly with her words. The moment she admitted her feelings he felt twenty-five again, young and able to conquer the world. With every beat of his heart he wanted only to caress her cheeks, kiss her lips, and find a way to love her like he was dying to do. But even in the heat of the moment he pictured his wife's face and shook his head.

He wasn't one of those men who easily had affairs. Never did he intend to cheat on Susan or do anything that would threaten their marriage. It simply wasn't in him to live a life of lies, spitting in the face of integrity and faithfulness. He framed the younger woman's face with his fingertips and spoke words that were almost impossible to say. "You're not in love with me, Leslie. You're lonely and you need a friend. That's easy to confuse."

Leslie's tears subsided and she apologized. But before she left that day, she kissed him on the cheek and said something that stuck with Mark every hour of every day for the next two months. "I'm not confused. If you weren't married, I'd take you home and show you the difference between love and friendship so you wouldn't have to wonder."

The images of those days disappeared.

Mark leaned back in his chair and locked eyes with Micah Phillips. "I thought I was being good, you know . . .

resisting her that day. But when I got home, Susan came unglued."

Of all nights, Susan chose that one to unload months of concerns that had been building between them. She admitted that she'd called the firm several times around midday, and each time he'd been at lunch with Leslie.

"When you're late, she's late. I've seen her car in the parking lot beside yours." Susan planted her hands on her hips and scowled at Mark, and he couldn't help but think how much she looked like her mother. The contrast between her appearance and Leslie's far lovelier one was striking.

"We work together."

"Don't lie to me." Susan rolled her eyes. "What's happening, Mark? I don't want to be the last to know!"

Again Mark thought of everything at stake: his marriage, his reputation, his desire to be faithful. He swallowed back the truth and smoothed a lock of hair off Susan's forehead. "Nothing's happening." He hoped the truth didn't show in his eyes. "Leslie and I work together, nothing more."

But two months later he and Leslie were walking out of a restaurant one afternoon when Leslie began poking Mark in the ribs, teasing him about his tie not matching his shirt. They were both laughing, basking in the exhilaration of being together.

They passed an alleyway, and suddenly the tension

between them was more than Mark could take. He gently took hold of her wrist and pulled her into the dark, narrow roadway. In one smooth motion he braced himself against the back of a brick building and drew her close. Before either of them could say anything, his lips found hers and they kissed in a way that Mark had only dreamed possible.

Breathless, their eyes full of questions, they studied each other, and with a hunger Mark had never known, they kissed again and again. Later that week, when their clandestine kisses were no longer enough to satisfy them, they skipped lunch and went to her apartment.

After that there was no turning back.

Week after week Leslie would wait until she was locked in his embrace and then raise the question that weighed on both their minds. "What about Susan?"

It was a question Mark was not yet ready to deal with. He would put a finger to Leslie's lips and whisper the only thing he knew to say. "I love you . . . give me time. One day we'll be together forever."

Again the memories cleared.

Mark twisted in his seat and felt concern in the eyes of the others in the group. "I still loved Susan very much. We had three children to raise and a lifetime of marriage ahead. But that didn't change how I felt about Leslie." He paused and raked his fingers through his hair. "I didn't know what to do; I cared about both of them."

He stared at the floor and resumed the story.

"I began worrying about Leslie, what she might do." He blinked, easily recalling the anxiety that beset him once his affair turned physical.

He remembered one day when he came home late from work after a long lunch at Leslie's apartment. His ten-year-old daughter met him at the door. "Daddy . . ."

There were tears in her eyes and Mark dropped to one knee in front of her. "What is it, honey? What's wrong?"

She batted her silky eyelashes and began to cry in earnest. "Do you still love us?"

Mark was unable to breathe. It was the same feeling he'd had once when he belly-flopped in the park pool and had the wind knocked out of him. He hugged his daughter tightly to his chest until he could find his voice. "Of course I love you."

She looked in his eyes, searching for childlike truth. "All of us?"

"Yes." Mark swallowed hard. "Every one of you."

"Then come home early like you used to, okay?" She wiped her tears and clung to Mark. "And once in a while eat lunch with Mommy. She misses you."

His daughter's words that day were enough to weight his decision. He had no business carrying on an affair with Leslie when the truth was he had no intention of leaving Susan and the kids. What if Leslie called Susan? What if she stopped by his house to visit him? What if Susan caught them together at the office? Or worse, at her apartment? The fears were enough to make him feel twice his age, and he knew that somehow, someway, the lying would have to end. Someone would have to lose, and he determined it wouldn't be Susan or him.

And it certainly wouldn't be their children.

Besides, this was Leslie's fault. She had practically thrown herself at him. If only he wasn't drawn to her every time she passed by his office door, if only her conversations didn't challenge him and make him feel vibrantly alive . . .

"No matter how I felt, I was planning to end things with Leslie." Mark locked eyes with Micah while the rest of the group listened intently. "I had no idea what was coming."

That week, Leslie came to his office early in the morning and again locked the door behind her—something she never did during business hours. Mark could see by her expression that something was terribly wrong.

"What is it?" He was on his feet and met her halfway across the room. His heart rate doubled and he wondered if somehow Susan had discovered their affair.

For a long while Leslie searched his eyes. Then she crossed her arms tightly in front of her and stared at the floor. "I'm pregnant."

In that instant, everything about Mark's measured life collapsed around him. He could feel the blood draining from his face; his heart lay mangled somewhere beneath his kneecaps. "I . . . I'm sorry."

Leslie's face went white. "You're *sorry?*" She huffed and paced across the office and back again. "You're sorry? Is that all you can say?"

Mark's mind raced almost as fast as his pulse. What was he supposed to say? He had a wife and three children at home. Any day now he was planning to end the affair with Leslie, encourage her to move on, find a man closer to her age. The last thing he'd expected was that she might not have been protected, that somehow in the midst of what was supposed to be a purely physical relationship she might get pregnant.

His knees knocked and he felt a row of perspiration break out across his forehead. "Leslie, I'm married." He dropped to his chair and anchored his elbows on his mahogany desk. He pictured his daughter's tear-stained eyes, the way they'd looked when she met him at the door that day. "I was . . . going to break things off with you this week."

She took three steps backward and leaned hard against his office door. "What?" The word was a pinched whisper. "I thought . . ." For a moment she appeared to melt several inches and Mark wondered if she might pass out. Then she found a fraction of her voice. "I thought you loved me."

His heart sounded the way his tennis shoes did when

Susan put them in the dryer. "I can't just walk away from my family." He huffed hard, unable to believe the disaster that had suddenly befallen him. "You're young. You'll be fine. But Susan . . . I'm all she has."

Leslie opened her mouth but no sounds came out. As beautiful as she was and as bad as he felt, Mark no longer found her attractive and compelling. Gone was the allure and electricity between them, the certainty that he couldn't go a day without holding her, kissing her.

All that remained was a feeling colder and darker than winter.

"I won't be fine." She stared at him, silent tears spilling from her eyes. "I loved you, Mark."

That was the last time he saw Leslie Landers alive.

Two days later, the partners called an emergency meeting and made the announcement. Leslie had been found by her elderly neighbor, dead in her apartment. There was an empty bottle of pills near her bed and a note on her dresser. It said only this:

"I'm sorry. I didn't know any other way out."

The news hit him like an eighteen-wheeler. Along with the others at the firm, he mumbled the appropriate words of shock and condolences. Then he barely made it to his office in time to collapse to his knees.

Mark stopped the story there and stared at the others. "How did it get so bad?" He linked his hands behind his head and stared at the ceiling, waiting for the lump in his throat to subside. "It seems like yesterday when Leslie walked into my office wanting nothing more than a conversation."

The whole time Micah had interjected nothing, letting him talk. But now, when no words could aptly describe the pain, Micah settled her fingers loosely over her clipboard and pursed her lips. "There's more, isn't there?"

A long, troubled breath emptied from Mark's lungs. "Yes." He forced himself to breathe, buried under the guilt of what had happened. "Before she died, Leslie called Susan and told her everything."

Micah's voice was quiet, sympathetic. "Susan and the children moved out with her mother the day after Leslie's funeral."

Mark nodded and suddenly the entire suit of protective armor he'd walked in with fell away. In its absence was a man who was no longer a hotshot attorney blithely sharing a story in front of a group of strangers. For the first time in his life Mark Adams had to admit the truth. He was something he'd never expected to be.

He was a cheater, a liar, a moral failure.

And he was a murderer.

The truth was more than he could bear and he doubled over, consumed with guilt and sorrow. Whatever magic Micah Phillips intended to work on him, he hoped it would happen soon. Because many more nights like this and Mark Adams knew something else.

He would have to find his own bottle of pills.

Micah typically tried to stay detached from situations discussed by the patients in her Heart-Crisis Intervention meetings. But watching Mark Adams cry, she found herself struggling as she hadn't in years. She allowed the appropriate five minutes, giving time for several other group members to place a hand on Mark's shoulder or knee. *I should be in his place*, she thought. Then she turned her attention back to the group.

"Who'd like to be next?"

Across from Mark Adams and seated beside Micah was a former schoolteacher in her midtwenties, Rhonda Willagher. When Mark got to the part in his story about his lover committing suicide, tears began tracking down Rhonda's face. Now that it was time for someone else to volunteer his or her story, Rhonda could no longer hold back.

She raised her hand, feeling like one of the third graders she used to have in class. Back before her teaching career was taken from her. Before everything good and pure and right about her life ended in utter disgrace.

Micah introduced her to the others and then nodded in her direction. "Take your time."

Rhonda ran her finger over the slight indent on her left ring finger, the place where her wedding band once was. If only Rick had been more interested in her . . . if he hadn't spent so much time at med school working toward his degree. Maybe if she'd felt even a little loved she wouldn't have been vulnerable to the advances of a—

She couldn't finish the thought.

"It started last year. We had no children and my husband, Rick, was busy. I was home alone a lot. Bored to tears. Finally, I offered to sponsor the high-school ski club." She uttered a sound that was part laugh, part cry. "The whole point was to do something positive with my time. Help out somehow."

Memories came like a flood, and she drifted back to the club's formation. Eighteen students signed up for what were supposed to be weekly meetings and a total of four ski trips, one an overnighter two hours north.

"I wasn't the only sponsor." Rhonda lifted her fingers off her lap and let them fall again. She tried to make eye contact with the group but only Mark Adams seemed to be listening intently. "Three of us were involved. Two men and myself. The whole thing seemed safe enough."

All but three of the students were boys, so the plan was set up-front. During trips, Rhonda would chaperone the girls. The men would handle the boys.

She remembered the first meeting like it was yesterday.

The students took their places, and last in was Skip Harrington, a strapping blond with bronze biceps, who didn't look a day under twenty-five years old. The sign-up sheet told the truth—he was seventeen, a straight-A senior involved in every sport at the high school. He grinned at Rhonda with flirtatious eyes and a shy, unforgettable smile. Then he walked to the front of the room and took a seat beside her.

He nodded politely. "You must be new."

Rhonda was twenty-four, and used to spending her days with grade-school children. Still, she was a professional and not inclined to encourage hormonal outbursts from students like Skip. She held out her hand and kept her expression serious. "Ms. Willagher. Ski Club sponsor. I teach at the elementary school down the street."

Skip pursed his lips and held out the palms of his hands. "Hi. I'm Skip."

When the meeting got underway, one of the men introduced the sponsors and told the students that Rhonda had once skied competitively. "She's good," the man told the group. "Watch her closely. You're bound to learn something."

A boy across the room whistled quietly. "I'll bet."

Skip said nothing, but Rhonda could see the corners of his mouth lift.

The memory stopped short.

"I wasn't expecting that kind of attention." Rhonda

looked at Micah and the others. "But I was so lonely, I guess I sort of liked it. So what if a few boys had a crush on me? What could it hurt?"

She continued the story.

The rest of that first meeting Skip made only the most appropriate comments. When other students teased her about looking like a high-school girl, he refrained. But at the end of the hour he waited until she was alone and came up beside her. "Hey . . ."

She turned to him and realized that he was six inches taller than her. "Yes?"

He smiled. "I'm glad you're a sponsor."

A lump formed in Rhonda's throat as she blinked back Skip's words. "No big deal, right?" She glanced at the faces in the counseling group and felt them agreeing with her. "So he tells me he's glad I'm a sponsor. What problem was that?"

She drifted back again and recounted how Skip's comment had haunted her all that night and into the week. She would be shopping at the grocery store, knowing that Rick wouldn't be home until well after ten o'clock, and Skip's words would ring in her head.

I'm glad you're a sponsor . . .

By the time they took their first day trip up the mountains, Rhonda was certain that Skip's attraction to her was more than a passing high-school crush. She was tightening her skis in the clubhouse that day when he came and sat beside her. "I'm supposed to watch you, right? Isn't that what they told us?"

She shrugged and remembered the seven years between them. *I'm the teacher; he's the student*, she told herself. But still she smiled. "I guess."

Skip angled his head, and his eyes shone in the light of the window. "I'll let you know what I think."

As it turned out, the three girls—all friends who never strayed from each other—were novice skiers. One of the male sponsors had a bad knee and offered to supervise them. "That's about all the speed I'm up to today," he told Rhonda. "You take the advanced boys. Make them ski first so you get an assessment of their skills."

For a moment Rhonda considered refusing. After all, even with a bad knee, Rhonda knew the male sponsor could have kept an eye on the advanced group. But Skip was in that set of skiers, and the thought of spending a day on the slopes with him was simply irresistible. Besides, she was supposed to ski with the students. That was her job.

There were four skiers in the advanced group. Rhonda rode the lifts up with them and watched each of them go down. Skip stayed at her side, and just before it was his turn he looked at her and grinned. "You go first."

She laughed, doing her best to maintain the teacher-student relationship between them. "You heard the instructions. Students first, then the sponsor. At least on the first run."

"But I'm supposed to watch you." He met her eyes and she felt their age difference fade. "I've been looking forward to that since our first meeting."

"Skip . . ." Her chin lowered and she raised her eyebrows. "Don't cause trouble. Take the run; I'll be right behind you."

Then without warning, he took her hand in his and pulled her toward the slope. "Come on . . . let's take it together." Momentum sent them both over the edge. When he spoke again, his voice was filled with exhilaration and laughter as he shouted above the rushing wind. "This way we can watch each other."

Down the mountain they soared and slalomed, side by side. At the bottom Rhonda found herself breathless, but not from the cold mountain air or the excitement of the run.

Because of Skip.

He was the most amazing skier she'd ever seen. Pure grace and athleticism in motion, so fluid and beautiful, he looked like a snow flurry dancing down the mountainside.

"They were right." Skip pulled up short beside her and dusted a smattering of snow off her cheek. "You're good."

"Yeah . . ." A short laugh came from her throat and jump-started her breathing. "You, too."

They skied together the rest of the day, and not till late that afternoon did Rhonda realize she'd lost track of the other students. Suddenly fearful that her attention toward

Skip might have caused a problem, she hurried to one of the male sponsors and checked in. Her heart skipped a beat in relief when she learned that everything was fine. No one had noticed how she spent her day.

At that week's meeting, Skip stayed after and asked if she had time to talk.

Rhonda looked at her watch and considered the situation. The door was open; no one could accuse her of anything less than appropriate. Besides, she and Rick had no children at home waiting for her, and with Rick's hours, she had no reason to leave. She took a seat, leaving three chairs between them. "Shoot."

Skip talked about how he didn't fit in with the other students at Jefferson High. Especially the girls. "They're so immature. It's like they're pretending to be grown up."

Rhonda smiled. "High school can be hard."

There was a comfortable silence between them for a beat. Then Skip's expression grew serious. "How come your husband lets you ski with a bunch of teenage guys?"

The empty places in Rhonda's heart felt glaringly obvious. She leaned back and studied him, a smile playing on her lips. "You're the student; I'm the teacher. You're not supposed to ask those questions."

He leaned over his knees. "I'm not *your* student." His eyes sparkled as he locked onto her gaze. "I'd say we're more like friends . . . wouldn't you?"

Rhonda thought about that. It was true in some ways. She taught children, third graders. And Skip was no child. He was more man than most men her age, if she was honest with herself. Besides, he paid her more attention than Rick had in years. "I guess. But still, it's better if—"

"That settles it." He stood up and grinned. "We're friends." He paused. "Now . . . can I say something else?"

She laughed and tossed her hands in the air. "You'll say it anyway."

He took two steps toward her and gently helped her to her feet. "I think your husband is crazy."

Again Skip's words stayed with her.

All that week when Rick was too tired to talk, too worn out for anything remotely intimate, Rhonda could think of nothing but Skip's observation. The boy had it bad for her, and Rhonda knew that staying clear of him was only one way to diffuse the situation. Still, there was no denying how good she felt in his presence.

Over the next two months and several ski trips, they spent more time together than ever, though Rhonda kept their growing friendship a secret, careful not to appear flirtatious or overanxious to ski with him. But something was happening between them, something irreversible.

No matter how wrong it was, she felt herself falling for him.

Rhonda stopped the story there.

A tear made its way down her cheek and she wiped it, sniffling twice and taking a tissue from Micah. "Even now it sounds disgusting. A twenty-four-year-old woman having feelings for a seventeen-year-old boy. But Skip was so much older than his age." She shrugged. "It wasn't something I planned. It just happened."

Skip turned eighteen the week before the overnighter.

Two days later one of the male sponsors called Rhonda. "I thought you should know that the girls pulled out. They decided not to go this weekend."

Rhonda felt a sense of alarm course through her. "Where does that leave me?"

"You're off the hook. You can stay home if you want." The man laughed. "I would if I had the choice. A semester with these kids is enough for me."

"Well . . ." Rhonda's mind raced. "I'm pretty much packed." She forced a lighthearted chuckle. "Actually I was kind of looking forward to it."

The man paused. "That's fine. I'm sure the kids'll be glad to have you." He hesitated and Rhonda heard the sound of shuffling papers. "I'll put you in a room by yourself on the other side of the advanced boys."

Ask him for a room somewhere else, in another wing, anywhere but near Skip . . .

The strange thought came and went in less than a second's time. What did it matter where her room was?

"That'd be great." Rhonda forced herself not to sound anxious. "See you Friday morning."

From the moment the group met in the school parking lot and loaded equipment on the school bus, Rhonda could feel the attraction between Skip and her growing. Their arms brushed against each other several times while they packed suitcases in the bus's luggage compartment. When it was time to leave, she was last on and took one of the only open seats—directly across from Skip.

"Who're you chaperoning?" His foot crossed the narrow aisle and tapped hers playfully.

"You." She kicked her toes back at his and tried to look serious. "Stay in line."

He winked at her, and they spent the rest of the ride talking about his dreams of being an accountant or a business mogul or a scientist. "With weekends off for skiing, of course." His eyes narrowed, locked on hers. "Then one day I'll marry someone just like you."

Rhonda tried to pretend she hadn't heard the comment but it was too late. Once again his words hit their mark, and by the time they settled in their rooms at the lodge and took to the slopes, she could think of nothing more than the fact that he was legally an adult.

And he was sleeping in the room next to hers.

Four hours later, after a dozen nighttime runs, the group turned in. But before Skip headed for his room, he found her by the coffee station and leaned close, his voice barely a whisper. "Meet me by the fireplace in two hours."

They were the longest two hours of her life.

She tried to remember the reasons she'd fallen in love with Rick. Before the trip, he had pulled her aside and apologized for his long hours.

"The hard work is almost over, honey," he told her. "I'll be a doctor next year at this time, and then we can have the life we always dreamed of. A house and babies and vacations at the beach." He kissed her on the forehead. "How can I ever thank you for standing by me all these years?"

As the two hours passed, she refused to dwell on Rick's parting words. Instead she remembered the lonely weeks and months without him. Rhonda stared out the hotel window and knew it didn't matter. She couldn't possibly have a relationship with Skip. He was a student after all, even if he was an adult. What did it matter if they spent an hour or so talking?

When it was time, she tiptoed from her room and made her way up two floors to the fireplace loft. Her husband's words and her fine-sounding arguments for avoiding Skip were as far removed as life outside the ski resort. All that mattered was how badly she wanted to spend time alone with Skip.

The room was completely empty except for a tall figure in the shadows.

"Hi." Skip stepped into the firelight and smiled as he made his way slowly toward her. He had two opened cans of beer and offered one to her. "I didn't think you'd come."

Rhonda listened intently, but heard nothing from the group below. She took the beer, feeling suddenly shy as she hung her head briefly and then made eye contact with him. She couldn't drink with a student on a school-sponsored trip. What would happen if they were caught? But then . . . everyone was asleep. Who would ever know?

He took a long sip, and she did the same. For a moment they drank in silence, her eyes locked on his. When the beer was more than half gone, she realized she didn't feel as shy as before, and she smiled. "I figured you wanted to talk."

"No, you didn't." Skip hesitated, inches from her. He finished his beer, tossed the can in a nearby trash bin, and wove his fingers through her hair. Then he took her face tenderly in his hands. Before Rhonda could think or speak or do anything to rein in her feelings, Skip leaned down and kissed her.

It took only a few seconds for Rhonda to jerk back and shake her head. "No! Skip, we can't. Someone will find out and . . ."

"Shhhh." He took the beer from her and held it to her lips. It was well past midnight, and the crackling fire was the only other sound in the lodge. When she had finished it, he kissed her again and again until she no longer had any intention of protesting. Until she was so caught up in the way his arms felt around her that she could barely breathe.

He drew back first, his eyes veiled in longing. "Let's go to your room."

Before she could think of a single reason why they shouldn't go, he grabbed what remained of a six-pack of beer, took her hand, and led her down two flights of stairs and through a back corridor that went straight to her room. Her hands trembled as she slipped the key in the door and followed him into the room. *We'll only talk and kiss, she told herself. Nothing more. An hour or so and it'll be over with.*

She blinked back the memory.

"Instead, it was like we both knew what was going to happen." Rhonda closed her eyes briefly, not wanting to see the shock on the faces of the group members. Even Micah Phillips had to be appalled at the awful story. She looked around the group. Instead of shock she saw empathy. They weren't judging her.

They understood completely.

She drew a deep breath and continued. "We drank some more and then we started kissing. I don't know how long it was before we moved to the bed." She dug deep down and found the courage to continue. "He was . . . he was on top of me and our shirts were off when it happened."

One of the male sponsors had been assigned to the adjacent room—the one where Skip was supposed to be.

Something must have woken him, and he realized Skip was missing. Because he was in charge of the group, he knocked at the door separating his room from Rhonda's.

When no one answered, he used a master key and opened it.

She and Skip didn't hear anything until the sponsor shouted at them. "Get off her!" The man walked up to Skip, grabbed him by the arm, and threw him on the floor. Then he glanced at the table and four empty beer cans. His face was beet red when he stared at Rhonda, his eyes narrow and angry. "Get dressed. Both of you meet me in the hallway in two minutes."

The moment they were alone again, Skip approached her and helped her to her feet. His face was whiter than the sheets. "I'm sorry, Rhonda. This is bad . . . this is really bad."

Rhonda couldn't speak. She slipped her shirt on, ran her fingers through her hair, and immediately went into the hallway to remedy the situation.

But it was too late.

She was ordered home a day early, and that Monday she was at the center of an emergency meeting with the high-school principal and superintendent. In less than an hour she was fired and told she could never work as a teacher anywhere in the state again. In addition, charges were pending by Skip's family.

"They treated me like a leper, like I had some contagious

disease, and if they came too close or talked too kindly, they might catch it." Sobs broke free, and Rhonda wept before the counseling group. There was no way she could finish the story. "Micah . . . tell them the rest."

Micah glanced at her clipboard and exhaled softly. "The boy wasn't a minor, so no crime was committed; however . . . ," she hesitated, "his family pressed civil charges against Rhonda for misusing her role as teacher and for consuming alcohol with their son and harming him in the process. The press found out and interviewed the male sponsors. The story ran on the front page of the local paper with photographs of Rhonda and Skip taken on earlier trips. Follow-up stories continued for a week afterward. The publicity was so bad she couldn't go to the grocery store without being recognized."

Rhonda blew her nose and nodded. "My husband moved out before the week was up. I haven't talked to Skip since."

Again there was silence while Rhonda cried and the others waited. "My mother made me come tonight. I . . . I told her I didn't want to live anymore. She was afraid for my life." Two quick sobs slipped from her throat. "I'm so afraid, Micah. Please . . . please give me a reason to live."

Micah felt a wave of panic work its way through her veins. "Answers will come later, Rhonda. Thank you for sharing."

There were still three stories ahead, and she wondered how much heartache she could take. Especially with all she had waiting for her at home.

She looked at the charts and considered the stories they were about to hear.

There was a man who had given up a wife and two children in pursuit of his position as president of a dot.com company. When the stock markets fluctuated shortly after the turn of the century, the man lost everything and tried to win his family back. But by then it was too late. His wife had remarried, his children no longer knew him, and his aging parents had died without his making peace with them.

Also in the circle was a woman who was facing five years in prison for swindling her company. She had concocted phony purchase orders and found a way to have the funds wired to her private account. In the process, she teamed up with the husband of her best friend—a man who also worked for the company. Now she was pregnant with his baby, and the two of them would most certainly serve time. The scandal had destroyed their futures, ruined a lifelong friendship, and devastated both families.

And finally a waitress who took a ride with a stranger, agreed to share coffee with him, then had to endure three hours of painful rape before crawling to a pay phone and calling her parents.

Micah gulped back the tears lodged in her chest.

The sad truth was that none of the stories or people that night really connected with her.

Not in light of her own story.

She pictured her son locked up in the state prison and remembered how it had started. *Mom, it's just pot. Everyone's doing it.*

Micah was a single parent, and her son's answer seemed sound enough at the time. After all, even doctors were prescribing marijuana for certain ailments. What harm was there if her son and his friends smoked pot now and then? Especially if they did it at her house? That way she could make sure they didn't drive intoxicated. She could offer them a safe place to sleep off the high.

But who could have guessed that her son would start dealing? Or that police would track the operation to her house and find out the truth . . . that she'd been contributing to the crime by allowing minor children to use drugs under her supervision?

By tomorrow everyone would know the story.

Her attorney had told her the facts as straight as he could make them. In the morning, police would most likely arrest her and though she might post bail, the press would hear about the charges. By week's end she would have lost everything.

Her son, her reputation, her career, and quite possibly her freedom.

All for what?

She clenched her fists and forced a smile. "Who's next?"

The stories poured out from her remaining participants, and suddenly the room was engulfed in an uncomfortable silence.

"Well . . ." Mark Adams chuckled from across the circle. His eyes settled on Micah. "Isn't this where you work your magic? I think we all need some answers."

Micah's mind worked fast and hard, searching through her bank of helpful words and calming advice, desperate for something that would give these people hope. She considered telling them the usual lines—that none of what had happened was their fault . . . that sometimes life threw curve balls, and that hopefully they could make up for their mistakes next time around. She could remind them that they were still worthy individuals, important people with a future ahead of them.

But an overwhelming sense of nausea washed over her and she stood. "Excuse me."

She ran from the room and barely made it to the toilet before vomiting. One of her patients found her there, crying in the stall.

"Are you okay?" It was Rhonda Willagher, and she stood just outside the door.

Micah cleared her throat. "Not really. Do me a favor . . ."

"Sure . . . anything."

"Tell them I'm sick. I'll make my evaluations and phone them with a recommendation in the next few days."

Rhonda hesitated. "Okay . . . Want me to call someone for you?"

Micah squeezed her eyes shut. There was no one to call. Nowhere to go but home, where, come morning, police would knock on the door and arrest her. "No. I'm fine."

Long after Rhonda was gone, after the other group members had made their way out of the parking lot, Micah stayed in the bathroom hovered over the toilet and weeping. Why hadn't she been able to finish the meeting? Life was full of problems, right? What was wrong with her? She should have been able to handle it like anyone else in the group.

A full hour later the reason finally came to her. She hadn't gotten sick because of her problems, but because of something far worse.

After a lifetime of dispensing advice, she'd gotten sick because of the terrifying truth.

Her standard answers, the ones she handed out every week, were nothing but patronizing clichés, memorized phrases without power or meaning. And that was something she hadn't realized until that moment. Something that made her afraid to move beyond the bathroom and back into the world.

Even if she found a way out of the legal disaster about

to beset her, she could no longer help the distraught masses that found their way into her counseling center. Not even if she wanted to. Because the reality was this: There were no answers.

Not for her or them or anyone else.

Quietly, trancelike, Micah Phillips, counselor to the most deeply troubled people in the city, made her way out of the bathroom to the sanctity of her private office. There she turned the dial on a safe beneath her desk and found a gun she'd purchased for protection. Once in a while truly wacky people made their way into her center, and she felt safe knowing the gun was within reach.

But the loaded weapon represented a different type of protection now. Safety from probing policemen and angry lawyers and an only son sitting in prison. Protection from a lack of answers that once made up her livelihood.

Protection from life itself.

She took a deep breath and thought about the people she would disappoint by making this decision. *It doesn't matter.* She thought of the stories that had played out that night. *Life is full of disappointments. This will merely be one more.*

The gun trembled in her hands. She touched the barrel to her temple and positioned her finger on the trigger. A minute passed and then another and she set the gun down. It was too soon to take her life. There was still a chance things might work out, wasn't there? Even if there were no answers, no sure things.

Her jagged breathing echoed in the empty room as she slipped the gun back in the safe and spun the dial. It would be there later, if things got bad enough.

And for now, that was the only sure thing that mattered.

PART
ONE

Heart
of the
Matter

I

Emotions:
The Language of the Heart

For out of the abundance of the heart the mouth speaks.
—MATTHEW 12:34

MICAH PHILLIPS WAS LIKE A LOT OF SECULAR counselors. She wanted to reach out to people and help them. But when her own world came crashing down, she realized that she didn't have any real answers. Her well-intended advice sounded hollow in light of the magnitude of her own problems.

The reason Micah Phillips had no answers for her distressed patients is simple: Her wisdom included no understanding of spiritual matters. And definitely no understanding of the importance of guarding one's heart.

If it had, she would have recognized a common thread between Mark Adams's story and that of Rhonda Willagher. The same thread that ran through her own life.

The thread was this: Each of them had made small, seemingly unimportant choices that led to an avalanche of devastation. In their own ways they traipsed the trail from discontent and distracted to deception and finally destruction.

All by allowing one bad choice to lead to another.

In other words, they were unable to guard their hearts, the control center for their emotions.

The next morning, Micah attended a Rotary Club breakfast where she sat across the table from Tom Thompson, a minister from a church in her community. He could see the distress on her face and asked if he could talk to her after the meeting.

Their conversation would lead to the greatest moment in Micah's life. She would soon discover that there really was hope after all.

WHAT OUR HEARTS ARE TELLING US

Emotions are the feelings that fuel our reactions to life's challenges. They can make us soar to the heights of happiness or plunge us into the depths of despair. Sometimes our emotions burst out abruptly and surprise us—like when we cry at a wedding, laugh at a funeral, or get angry over a hairbrush.

Emotions can make a person say or do things he or she will regret for a lifetime. They can dent a friendship, damage a relationship, or destroy a marriage. Out of control, emotions can become the most destructive force in the world. Yet, properly guarded, emotions can be a powerful force for good.

We can't always control the initial outbursts of emotion, but we can learn to deal with them. If we don't, our emotions may destroy our relationships with family and friends. Ultimately they will destroy us, too, if we let them.

In essence, we choose whether the choices of our hearts will result in destruction or lead us to victory in all matters of emotions.

Silvan Tomkins, a brilliant psychological theorist and researcher, has studied various cultural, racial, and ethnic groups, observing that all people have common facial features when expressing any one of nine different emotions.[1] These emotions are common to the human experience regardless of cultural differences. In commenting on this factor, Christian psychologist Dan Allender remarks:

> Tomkins discovered what God implied when he said to Cain, "Why are you angry? Why is your face downcast?" (Genesis 4:6).

In simple terms, the inner world "communicates" the disposition of the soul to others through the expression on the face. But the outer world often does not wish to hear or see the state of our souls, therefore, emotion is suppressed, distorted, and denied. It loses its intensity but not its reality. We can no more avoid emotion than we can escape thought, choice or desire. It is wired into us.[2]

Emotion is our primary motivating force. It propels our personalities, decisions, choices, and values. More and more, psychologists are coming to realize that emotions are often the cause of our behavior as well as the result of our behavior. Only when we realize that our emotions are related to our hunger for God and what He can provide can we begin to understand our own wrestling match with God. Allender observes that our emotions express our frustration with God and yet invite us to surrender to God. "We are to struggle with God until our heart surrenders to his goodness," he writes. "The proper focus of emotion is God. Once we see that struggling with God is not a sign of spiritual deficiency, but spiritual depth and hunger that drive us to taste the goodness of God . . ."[3]

Christian psychologist Larry Crabb describes spirituality as "that profound engagement with God that establishes identity, ignites love, and releases uniqueness."[4] He points out that counselors sometimes bypass true spirituality in their hurry to solve the very problems God may be using to drive people closer to Himself. It is here in the depth of the human heart that we meet God personally.

We see this illustrated over and over again in the terrorist attacks on New York City. Countless people stand at "Ground Zero" staring at the ruins of the World Trade Center. They are looking for answers to their deepest hurts. Searching for hope, they often turn to God.

One of the most unusual experiences of our time has been the spiritual awakening that has come to America in the days following the terrorist attacks. People have spontaneously truned to God while the secular culture has remained silent because it has no answers for the human heart.

UNDERSTANDING YOUR HEART

The term *heart* is used in the Bible both literally and metaphorically. In some passages, it refers to the actual organ of the body. But most of the time, it refers to the seat of our emotions and the source of our spiritual life.[5] In the Old Testament, the Hebrew word for "heart" is *leb*. It refers to the spiritual, intellectual, and emotional nature of human beings. But it is more than a description of isolated functions. *Leb* refers to the totality of a person and his or her inner life and character. Jeremiah 17:9 warns, "The heart is deceitful" and "desperately wicked." Yet, it is in the heart that worship and conversion to God take place (Psalm 51:10; Joel 2:12; Jeremiah 32:40).

The New Testament uses the Greek word *kardia* 148 times to describe the inner life of thinking, feeling, and willing. God is pictured as the "knower of hearts" (Greek, *kardiognostes*), a term unknown in secular Greek. The New Testament emphasizes that God alone knows the human heart and He alone can reveal what is in it (1 Corinthians 4:5; Romans 8:27; 1 Thessalonians 2:4). It is in the "heart" that God is known, that His word is revealed, and the peace of God begins to rule (Romans 6:17; Luke 8:15; Colossians 3:15). The New Testament describes the "true heart" as the one the blood of Christ cleanses (Hebrews 10:22) and the one in which He dwells by faith (Ephesians 3:17).

To the Hebrew mind, *heart* expresses the inward psychological and spiritual condition of a person as a condition of the heart. In the area of emotion, the heart may be hateful (Leviticus 19:17) or loving (Deuteronomy 13:3), sad (Nehemiah 2:2) or glad (Proverbs 27:11). In more than three hundred cases, *heart* refers to spiritual significance in describing one's relationship to God.[6] The "right heart" is a result of God's gracious spiritual activity to bring permanent and lasting change into our lives.

Biblical scholar Walter Elwell says, "The heart is especially important in biblical religion."[7] In Christian terms, spiritual transformation involves believing the gospel from a "noble" and "good" heart (Luke 8:15). Elwell adds, "The true heart draws near to God, loves him with all its intellect, feeling, and will (Luke 10:27; Hebrews 10:22). Then God becomes to the heart strength, reward, renewal, grace, peace, and joy (Psalm 78:26; Isaiah 57:15). So the ancient ideal becomes possible again, that of being 'a man after God's own heart'" (1 Samuel 13:14; Acts 13:22).[8]

The heart can be totally devoted (Deuteronomy 4:29) or it can be "bewitched" or "stolen" (Song of Solomon 4:9).[9] God told the ancient Hebrews to love Him with all their heart, soul, and strength (Deuteronomy 6:5). Later, He explained that He was looking for a man after His own heart to rule Israel (1 Samuel 13:14; 16:7). He explained that He "searches all hearts" to reveal their true motives (1 Chronicles 28:9). In repentance, the psalmist wrote, "Create in me a clean heart, O God" (Psalm 51:10). "Search me, O God, and know my heart," he prayed (Psalm 139:23).

Knowing God and serving God are activities described in the Bible as being done with "all your heart" (Proverbs 3:5). God promises, "You will seek Me and find Me, when you search for Me with all your heart" (Jeremiah 29:13). The apostle Paul said, "That if you confess with your mouth, 'Jesus is Lord,' and believe in your heart that God raised him from the dead, you will be saved" (Romans 10:9 NIV).

HEART AND SOUL

Several years ago, there was a popular booklet by Robert Boyd Munger entitled *My Heart—Christ's Home.*[10] In it, Munger described the believer's heart like the rooms of a house. "After Christ entered my heart," he wrote, "I said to Him, 'Lord, I want this heart of mine to be yours. I want you to settle down here and be perfectly at home. Everything I have belongs to you.'"[11] The author then proceeded to describe the "rooms" of his heart: (1) library (mind); (2) dining room (appetite); (3) drawing room (fellowship); (4) workshop (service); (5) recreation room (activities); (6) hall closet (secret sins).

After describing his attempts to clean up the rooms of his heart, the author realized: "I start on one room and no sooner have I cleaned it than another room is dirty. I begin the second room and the first room becomes dirty again."[12] Suddenly, he realized he needed to transfer the title for the entire house over to the Lord. Once his heart was totally surrendered to Christ, he found the key to a successful Christian life.

The missionary statesman Hudson Taylor's "spiritual secret" was the realization that "Christ is all." He said, "The Lord Jesus received is holiness begun; the Lord Jesus cherished is holiness advancing; the Lord Jesus counted on as never absent would be holiness complete."[13] Once Hudson Taylor learned that Christ was everything, he learned that abiding, not striving, was the secret of spiritual power. Dr.

Roy Aldrich writes, "It was this experience, this new apprehension of the sufficiency of Christ for everything, that ushered Hudson Taylor into his great life of spiritual power and missionary accomplishment."[14]

The heart is the emotional center of our lives. It is neurologically connected to every organ of your body. If the emotional center is disturbed, you will be upset and bothered by virtually everything. But if the emotional center of our beings is controlled by the Holy Spirit, we can experience His fruit of love, joy, peace, and patience. Everything our hearts desire for personal fulfillment can be provided by God. He alone can fill the vacuum of the empty human heart and fill it with the power and presence of God.

Spiritual growth is the result of the Spirit's work in our lives. Without Him, we can only attempt to develop a heart for God by the best self-effort we can muster. Otherwise, spiritual growth results from seeking God with all our hearts.

THE CHALLENGE

The only theological argument for which there is no debatable lack of evidence is the depravity of the human heart. Theologian W. G. T. Shedd writes, "An evil heart, if not restrained by divine grace, is certain to act wrongly."[15] The unregenerate heart lacks the capacity for eternal spiritual good. It may produce good thoughts or even good deeds, but without the power and presence of God, it cannot do anything to merit eternal life. The biblical solution to human depravity is divine regeneration—the heart must be "born again" by the power of God (John 3:3).

The new birth transforms the human heart. The Bible promises that God will give us a "new heart" and a "new spirit" (Ezekiel 36:26). But even this transformed heart must be restrained from wandering away from God. For most believers, our spiritual conversion was a high point in our lives. We came face to face with the claims of Christ and believed that He was the Savior and trusted Him explicitly. Our hearts were ignited with a divine passion for God. We came alive spiritually and wanted the whole world to know it. Whatever you call it—conversion, salvation, regeneration—it is the beginning of a brand new-life in Christ.

A beginning. A new start. A new life. But it is just the beginning. The lifelong process of spiritual growth and maturity (theologians call it *sanctification*) only begins at that point. Most of us don't realize it at the time, but we have just embarked on a long journey—a journey of the heart. Something down deep inside us told us this was it—the truth about God—as we believed it. Our hearts were set ablaze by God's presence in our lives.

As time passed and the journey progressed, we soon realized that there were many challenges ahead. The road of life is meant to be traveled, but sometimes it can get rough.

It can lead to excitement and adventure, or it can lead to failure and despair. Life is never all joy and no sadness. It is never success without failure or gain without pain. No matter what your spiritual experience, there will be obstacles to face and pitfalls to avoid.

Everybody has problems; we can't get far on the road of life without encountering them. No matter how much personal preparation you have made for the journey, there will be challenges to face about which you have never dreamed. Problems will have to be dealt with and decisions will have to be made. Some of these will determine the course of your life.

Starting the race is one thing—finishing it is another. That's where your heart may well determine the outcome. If you look up the word *heart* in a Bible concordance, you will find over three hundred references to the "heart" as the inner being of men and women. You will discover that it can be softened or hardened, impassioned or cold, yielding or resistant, broken or unrepentant. For believers, the constant appeal of Scripture calls us to love, worship, serve, and obey God "with all your heart" (Deuteronomy 6:5). Anything less falls short of true devotion to God.

FACING LIFE'S TOUGHEST PROBLEMS

The message of the Bible is one of help for the hurting. In its pages are the greatest resources in all the world. These timeless truths have stood the test of endurance generation after generation. Instead of new theories and experimental attempts, the Bible offers solid advice based upon the inspired truths of the Word of God. These truths tell us that God alone can and will help us deal with our problems.

While we experience the blessings of God in our daily lives, life is not without its difficulties, challenges, and struggles. The Bible reminds us that God comforts us *in* our troubles, not necessarily *from* our troubles (2 Corinthians 1:4). In fact, suffering and trouble are His methods of shaping our lives and our characters. In some cases, God may use the worst of circumstances to accomplish the best of results for our own good.

The Bible reminds us that God is greater than our problems. Since He rules the universe, He can overrule every circumstance of life for our own good. Romans 8:28 reminds us, "We know that in all things God works for the good of those who love him, who have been called according to his purpose" (NIV).

In our human weakness, we want to run from problems, while God wants to use those problems for our own good. The very fact that you are going through a difficult time may be the greatest indication that God is at work in your life. Rarely do we learn the deep lessons of life when everything is going well.

The real learning comes when everything goes wrong!

That's when God usually gets our attention. When the bottom falls out of our lives and there is nowhere else to turn, we will find ourselves instinctively calling on God for help. There is something basic to human nature that drives us to God when we come to the end of ourselves. Even unbelievers will cry, "God, help me!" when faced with a crisis.

TAKING THE FIRST STEP

How we handle our problems is the key to overcoming them. Our reaction will determine whether our problems become opportunities for personal growth or the means of spiritual and emotional defeat. Learning how to handle life's problems with the *right heart attitude* is the first step in overcoming them.

Wrong attitudes express our inner frustration with life and our bitterness toward God for allowing problems to come into our lives in the first place. They are symptoms of our refusal to believe that God is really in control of our lives. Ultimately, wrong attitudes push us away from God instead of drawing us to Him.

Running from God is like running away from the one person who can really help you. The more you run, the more He will pursue you like the "hound of heaven." His grace will keep reaching out to you even when you don't want it. Hebrews 6:19 reminds us that Jesus Christ is our "hope as an anchor for the soul, firm and secure" (NIV). This passage goes on to explain that He has anchored us to the heart of God, beyond the veil into the Holy of Holies in heaven itself. You may have run far enough to pull the links of the chain to their limit, but God will not let you go if you belong to Him.

The tug in your heart is the pull on the chain of the anchor of hope. That restless dissatisfaction in your soul is the stirring of the spirit to draw you back to the God who loves you. Your unwillingness to let go of Him is the evidence of His grace in your life. He has not given up on you. In fact, He may have just begun His greatest work in you.

We begin conquering our problems when we face them. As long as we deny that we have a problem, we will never really deal with it. Whether we realize it or not, most of our problems are the result of our own sinful responses to life's challenges. Only when we face those sins and admit them will we take responsibility to correct them. The Bible calls this process confession and repentance (Luke 13:3; 1 John 1:9).

The basic procedure for dealing with most of life's problems is relatively simple:

1. Face reality. Stop pretending things are fine when they are not. Denial will keep you from dealing with your problems. It may make you feel better for a while, but it will not solve your problems. The sooner you face reality, the better your chances of recovery.

2. Take responsibility. Be willing to take action to deal with your own problems. No one else can solve your problems for you. They can encourage, help, and support you in your crisis, but ultimately only you can take the responsible steps of action to correct your own problems.

3. Do right. There is a right way and a wrong way to handle every problem. Find the right way and do it! God's Word will guide you. It specifically tells us how to handle life's toughest problems.

TRUSTING GOD TO HELP US

Much of the New Testament deals with crises. Several letters (epistles) were written specifically to deal with problems like divorce, lawsuits, sickness, death, divisions, heresies, immorality, disorder, and marriage and family problems. There is hardly a problem today that Christians face that is not covered in the pages of Scripture. If we really want to know God's will for our lives in dealing with a particular problem, the Bible will guide us to the answer. Consider the experience of Brad and Julie.

"I thought I was doing the right thing," Brad said. "We needed the money, and I didn't intend to keep working at that pace forever. Before I knew it, Julie took the kids and moved in with one of her friends."

Brad explained that he had been working out of town

six days a week for nearly two years. Sometimes he was gone as much as three weeks at a time. Julie felt neglected and unloved. Her pleas to him seemed to go unanswered, so one day she and the children left.

"What can I do to get her back?" Brad asked. "I never meant for it to end like this!"

Brad and Julie's story is not unusual. In fact, it is all too often a reality for today's couples struggling with the pressures of modern life. Decisions about marriage, work, and family are often made with little regard for biblical teaching on these matters, which is so essential for effective and successful living.

The key to handling our emotions is learning to trust what God tells us to do about them. Too many people want to make their own decisions and then ask God to "bless" what they have already decided. Instead, we need to figure out what God wants us to do and do it with the confidence that He will bless it. Our obedience to His commands places us in a position to receive His blessings in our lives.

Our willingness to trust God in every circumstance of life depends on our confidence in His love. All uncertainty on our parts is an expression of distrust in His love. It is a basic rejection of God's character and nature. When we fail to trust Him with our problems, we are really distrusting His sincerity and integrity. Because He truly is an all-loving God with our best interests in mind, we must learn to trust His love for us in spite of our circumstances.

FINDING HIS PURPOSE IN IT ALL

Brad and Julie's marital crisis caused a temporary separation, but it also got their attention focused in the right direction. They stopped pretending everything was all right and finally did something about it. It wasn't easy, but they started doing what they should have been doing all along—honestly talking about their feelings, praying together, and seeking the kind of biblical counseling that could help them put things back together. In time they were able to deal with their problems head-on and solve them.

Whether we fully understand it or not, God is sovereign over the events in our lives. No matter how bad the crisis may appear to be, it is never beyond His ability to resolve it. Every crisis in our lives is part of God's sovereign purpose for us. We may not understand that purpose while we are going through the struggle, but we will eventually see how the circumstance was for our benefit.

This basic trust, so often overlooked in popular Christian self-help psychology books, is fundamental to any proper understanding of life's problems from a distinctively Christian viewpoint. If God is really present, then we are not alone in dealing with our problems. If His sovereign will prevails over these problems, then there are three things of which we can be certain:

1. God limits our problems. God is in control of our lives, and He limits the extent and duration of the crisis. God limited Satan's attack in the case of Job (1:12; 2:6). Jesus warned Peter that Satan would "sift" him as wheat, but assured Peter that He had prayed for his restoration (Luke 22:31–32). The Bible makes it clear that nothing can touch us that is beyond the limits of God's sovereign control.

2. God brings meaning to our problems. The problems of life are not tragic episodes in the absurd saga of human existence. There is purpose and meaning to our struggles, problems, and sorrows. Romans 8:18 promises "that our present sufferings are not worth comparing with the glory that will be revealed in us" (NIV). There is something meaningful in our problems . . . because there is a point to it all: God is in the crisis!

3. God assures us of His grace. There is no problem in life that is beyond the grace of God. He will help us in our time of need. When the apostle Paul struggled with his "thorn in the flesh," God assured him, "My grace is sufficient for you, for My strength is made perfect in weakness" (2 Corinthians 12:9). The Bible also tells us, "Cast all your anxiety on him because he cares for you" (1 Peter 5:7 NIV). God's grace is sufficient for every problem we face.

MAKING THE COMMITMENT

The biblical concept of faith is that of a deep personal commitment that leads to a step of action on our parts. The Bible never defines faith as mere intellectual assent. Nowhere in Scripture do we find people merely giving God an affirming nod. Real faith involves a total commitment of one's self to God.

When a person is genuinely converted, he or she believes the promise of God to the point of surrendering his or her life to Him. We may not understand every nuance of that commitment, but we know that we have believed the gospel to the point that it has resulted in a life-changing commitment to Jesus Christ.

That same kind of commitment is necessary in trusting God to help us with our emotions and resulting problems. We have always been amazed that people will trust God to forgive their sin and give them eternal life and a home in heaven, but they will not trust Him to help them with their problems here and now.

Halfhearted commitments will not help you solve your problems. Either God can help you or He can't. Either you trust Him or you don't. It is that simple. Most of us try to complicate matters by assuming the solutions to our problems have to be more complex. But Jesus simply said, "Come to me, all you who are weary and burdened, and I will give you rest. Take my yoke upon you and learn from me, for I am gentle and humble in heart, and you will find rest for your souls" (Matthew 11:28–29).

The key to handling our problems is learning to trust God with them. If we don't do that, we won't solve our problems. And if we won't commit our problems to God, we won't grow in His grace. We will remain stuck in our own self-absorbed indecision and inability to solve our problems.

Imagine if Mark Adams had followed his heart's first instincts and refused an improper friendship with Leslie Landers. What if Rhonda Willagher had stepped down from her position as ski club sponsor and chosen to spend her time drawing closer to God instead? In both cases, what if they'd chosen to invest their emotions and their hearts in their marriages instead of in outside distractions?

Remember, distractions make us vulnerable to deception and lead us down a path that often ends in destruction. But we won't be distracted if only we operate our hearts from a point of faith.

Faith is not a blind leap into the dark. Faith is believing the principles of God's Word and ordering our lives accordingly. God tells us how to live successfully. He doesn't leave us in the dark regarding His will for our lives. He spells it out for us in the Bible. The ultimate question is: *Do you trust God or don't you?* The answer to that question will determine how you handle life's toughest problems. You can do it your way . . . or you can do it His way.

Tom Thompson explained all of this to Micah Phillips and invited her to turn her life over to God.

"Right now?" Micah asked?

"Is there any reason you shouldn't turn to Him right now?" Tom replied.

Micah thought for a moment about her professional associates. What would they think? But her pain was so great and her need was so deep that she brushed all that aside. After all, she knew they didn't have the answers any more than she did.

"You're right," Micah sighed. "It's time. I'm ready to give my life to Him."

Tom took Micah's hand and suggested that they pray together. She opened her heart and the words flowed out of her as though they had been there all along—pent up by some wall of resistance.

"God, I know that I have failed You," Micah sobbed. "Please forgive me for pushing You away all these years. I do believe that Jesus died for my sins, and I want to trust Him as my personal Savior."

It was the first step in a brand-new life of faith for Micah. For the very first time, she felt there really was hope for the future. In the weeks that followed, Micah's newfound faith gave her the confidence to go back and face her clients. Now she had something to tell them that could really help each one of them find the forgiveness they needed.

2

The Battle
for the Heart

Above all else, guard your heart,
for it is the wellspring of life.
—PROVERBS 4:23 NIV

JASON AND HEATHER HAD BEEN MARRIED FOR SIX years when she came home one day and told him she was leaving. The shock and devastation rocked Jason's world. "I . . . I thought we were doing better." He met Heather near the front door and placed his hands gently on her shoulders. "Don't leave now. Please."

"Stop!" Heather spun around and stared out the window of their two-story home. "I can't stay. I can't live like this anymore."

Jason's mind raced. What had happened? Why was she

ready to leave when he thought they were doing fine? "I didn't think it was that bad."

She kept her back to him, but he could tell she was crying. "You have no idea how I feel."

"You should have told me." Jason kept his voice quiet, calm. Whatever this was, they could work it out. There was no point yelling at each other. "We can't be close if we don't talk."

"Close?" she said sarcastically. "We are as far apart as two people can get."

Jason's heart skipped a beat. What if she was serious? "You don't really believe that, do you?"

"I don't know." Heather hung her head and turned slowly back toward Jason. "My heart's cold. I feel like our love died months ago." She looked up, and fresh tears filled her eyes. "Want the truth?"

Jason swallowed hard. "Of course."

She sighed and stared at the worn carpet between them. "Lately I've been wishing I was married to someone else . . . someone like Scott."

There was silence for a moment and Jason clenched his teeth. How dare she pull this on him now? After he'd invested months of effort in staying married. "Scott!" His voice bounced off the plaster walls and he rattled a string of expletives. "Are you having an affair?"

"Not yet." She wiped her tears and met his gaze. "But I can't lie to you, Jason. I don't love you anymore."

Jason felt his world unraveling around him, and he sucked in a quick breath. "What about your parents?" He paced to the door and back. "They don't believe in divorce."

"Neither do I." Heather's voice rang with sincerity and sorrow. Suddenly Jason knew it was too late. Whatever they'd done to save their marriage, it wasn't enough. Heather took a step closer and reached for Jason's hand. The resolve in her eyes was frightening. "I can't go on like this, Jason. I'm leaving; I'm sorry. We can work out the details later."

Then, without another word, she picked up her bags and walked out of a marriage that was supposed to last forever.

Jason and Heather are like a lot of couples today. They grew up in Christian homes, attended church, and fell in love. Early on, romance swept them off their feet and thrust them into a fairy-tale relationship that culminated in marriage. But now, six years later, the fairy tale is over. Slowly, imperceptibly, they have drifted apart.

The reasons are as subtle as sin.

Jason was highly respected in his position as a computer programmer. But he brought his work home with him and spent most evenings glued to a glowing computer screen. Heather would beg him to spend an hour or two with her. But promises of five minutes, then ten, turned into an hour or two, and many nights Heather went to bed alone.

"He loved that machine more than me," Heather said later.

No wonder she was vulnerable to Scott's advances. Heather felt lonely and neglected, and as the months wore on she began thinking about other men. About that time, Jason and Heather attended a movie about a couple who broke up and found new lives and new hope with someone else. She couldn't get that image out of her mind. It wasn't long until she began seeing Scott, and the rest was as predictable as spring.

HEART WARS

The battle for the heart begins deep within the soul. Our inner emptiness cries out for something more, and the world rushes in to fill it. For some, it is an addiction. For others, it is a relationship. But whatever it is, it begins to draw us away from God. At first we try to resist it. But eventually we embrace it and lose all sense of spiritual restraint. Some embrace a new experience, a new idea, or even a new religion. Our guilty consciences tries to protest, but we soon make a mental or emotional paradigm shift and start defending a lifestyle we once rejected.

Dr. Gary Collins suggests that we have become a "nation of strangers" who are characterized by isolation and disconnection.[1] We rush from place to place and build our lives around one-way emotional attachments with the faces of our television and computer screens. Collins observes,

"This increasing isolation has been linked with a century-long withdrawal from religion."[2] Slowly, God has been shunted aside; cynicism and distrust have emerged as dominant lifestyles. Morals have become relative, leaving vulgarity and violence to run rampant.

The soul of American society is empty and rootless. Instead of driving us back to God, this emptiness pushes us to fill the voids in our hearts with food, sex, celebrities, and consumer products. Advertisers, professional helpers, exploitive therapists, corrupt politicians, money-hungry marketers, and even some religious leaders offer us an array of harmful solutions that only encourage our self-indulgence.

Dr. Collins says, "Having rejected God and traditional religion, too many people search for a new connectedness and fulfillment."[3] Eventually, millions of empty people turn to new relationships and even new spiritualities, trying to connect with some cosmic whole that will bring meaning and vitality into their lives. But these temporary highs only lead to greater emotional and spiritual lows that leave the hearts and souls of men and women even more vulnerable to Satan's devices.

Dr. D. James Kennedy suggests that the anti-Christian bias of television, movies, and the media are slowly eroding the morals and beliefs of Christians as well as non-Christians. He writes, "If Christians are portrayed at all, they are characterized as fanatics, hypocrites, extremists, ignoramuses, uneducated and bigoted."[4] But not only are the media guilty of misrepresenting religion in general, but for denigrating Christian morality in particular. Don Wildmon reports that 88 percent of sexual activity in prime-time television is between people who are not married, thus making "lust more attractive than love."[5]

Hollywood has paved the way for an open assault on Christianity and its morals and values. This has led to an all-out war against Christianity in the pop culture of our times. Movies, television, and music all join forces to denigrate Christian beliefs, morals, and values. The impact of this combined force is corrupting society and weakening our churches. Every element of our social fabric is being ripped apart by this demonic assault on the hearts of the men and women of our generation.

CANDY COAT THE APPEAL

The Bible warns us to "guard" our hearts because our hearts are so vulnerable to deception. The world's appeal to the heart often bypasses the rational processes of the mind. We can watch a television program or a movie that does this so effectively that we find ourselves cheering for the moral opposite of what we claim to believe.

The Oscar-nominated movie *Chocolat* is a perfect example.[6] The story is set in a small French village in the

1950s. The plot revolves around the moral leader of the community, a staunchly Catholic mayor, and a free-spirited woman who deliberately opens a chocolate shop at the beginning of Lent, in opposition to his religious protests. Almost immediately, the viewer is encouraged to side with the antireligious chocolatier. Before long, she allures the entire community to side with her. In the end, even the mayor and the parish priest cave in to her allurements.

The movie is highly entertaining and very well acted. But it definitely sends a powerful subliminal message that religion is far too moralistic and ought to lighten up and embrace all people as spiritual equals, even if they have no religious beliefs at all. At a crucial point in the story, the mayor observes, "What could be more harmless than chocolate?" But it was the seeming innocence of chocolate that gave the woman the opportunity to spread her message of an irreligious lifestyle in such an entertaining manner that the viewer is compelled to take her side as the story develops.

Our hearts are rarely tempted by the onslaught of evil in its most brazen and despicable forms. Such assaults offend our moral sensibilities, and we tend to reject them outright. But what does tempt us is the gradual allure of small departures of the heart. A little indulgence here or there is tolerable enough to excuse without bombarding ourselves with guilt. Slowly but surely, each little departure takes us further and further away from the purity of heart

God intends for us. Things once viewed as outrageous behavior are now quite commonplace in our society. That which used to shock us no longer causes anyone to blush.

The process of the gradual shift of society works like this: The believer's heart is fixed on knowing, loving, and pleasing God. But eventually the allurements of this life place our focus off God and onto ourselves. Our original spiritual passion diminishes, and we excuse it as a normal process of balancing our spiritual lives with our everyday responsibilities. Soon the focus of our hearts shifts even further away from God. We find ourselves obsessed with the cares of life—family, friends, business, activities, investments, and our eventual retirement. But somehow, in it all, we lose our passion for God. We still go to church. We pray. We talk about the Bible. Our lives are filled with Christian friends. But the dynamics of a personal daily walk with God begin to take a backseat to our other concerns—that is, until a crisis occurs that drives us to our knees and back to God. But if no such crisis comes along, it is possible to drift away from God and not even realize it.

THE BLAME GAME

Jason and Heather eventually agreed to talk to their pastor about their marital conflicts.

"Jason can't make me happy," Heather told the pastor at their first meeting.

Then he asked the question that hit at the core of the couple's problems. "How are you doing spiritually?"

"I'm fine." Heather looked at Jason and shrugged. "We're both fine."

When he pressed the issue further, Heather grew defensive. "What does *my* spiritual life have to do with Jason and our marriage?" she asked.

Before the pastor could answer, Heather launched into a tirade about Jason's inability to leave his job at the office.

"Wait a minute." Jason's voice rose a notch. "What about Scott? If you're seeing another man, you can't expect me to change for you."

The pastor asked them both to listen for a moment. Then he told them about the blame game. Blaming others is one way to shift attention away from our own responsibilities for our behavior. One of the major reasons people cannot handle the problem of temptation is their refusal to face the real source of their temptation: themselves! We must face the fact that we are our own worst enemies. The real source of temptation is neither God nor Satan. In most cases, temptation begins in our hearts as we are enticed to give in to our own desires. All too often, the Christian believer refuses to admit to himself that he is toying with sin—until it is too late.

The easiest way to avoid personal responsibility regarding our own sin is to blame it on the devil. Many people claim that they cannot deal with their temptation because "the devil made me do it."

One well-meaning lady told her counselor that she really didn't yell and scream at her husband. "The devil does it."

Her counselor replied, "I can't make the devil stop yelling at your husband, but I can ask *you* to stop."

Remember, Satan is not omnipresent; he is a limited, created being. Chances are that Satan has never dealt with you personally. Also, a believer is no longer under Satan's control. While he may trouble you from without (and that only by God's permission—see Job 1:12), he no longer has a claim over your life. His power has been broken by the victorious death and resurrection of Christ. Try as he might, Satan cannot enter your mind and possess your will, thought, or emotions.

We blame each other and the devil, and when we get truly desperate, we blame God. We may say, "Why is God doing this to me?"; however, the Bible clearly teaches that God is not the author of temptation: "When tempted, no one should say, 'God is tempting me.' For God cannot be tempted by evil, nor does he tempt anyone" (James 1:13 NIV).

God may allow Satan to tempt us, but even then the Bible promises that "God is faithful; he will not let you be tempted beyond what you can bear" (1 Corinthians 10:13 NIV). There is no excuse, then, for failure or defeat. Should we fail, we have only ourselves to blame. If God let temptation come to men such as Abraham, Job, Moses, David, and Paul, why should we expect to be exempt?

THE BATTLE BEGINS IN YOUR MIND

The Bible tells us plainly that what we think (Greek, *logizomai)* not only determines how we live, but reflects who we are. "For as [a man] thinketh in his heart, so is he" (Proverbs 23:7 KJV). Everyone knows what it is to be enslaved to lust, hatred, greed, jealousy, or envy. All of these are poison to the soul. Recognizing this, the apostle Paul wrote, "Finally, brothers, whatever is true, whatever is noble, whatever is right, whatever is pure, whatever is lovely, whatever is admirable—if anything is excellent or praiseworthy—think about such things" (Philippians 4:8 NIV).

Seven guidelines will help you clean up your thought life:

1. Admit that you have a problem. Rationalizing sin will never cure it. Whatever sinful thoughts trouble us, we must confess them to God. Be honest with Him who searches our hearts and minds and knows our thoughts. Read 2 Samuel 12 or Psalm 51, and learn the importance of laying your sin before God.

2. Believe that God can make a difference in your thought life. There are no doubting victorious Christians.

In Hebrews 11:6 we learn that without faith we cannot please God; if we are to approach Him for strength or wisdom, we must believe Him capable of supplying it. "Blessed be the Lord, who daily bears our burden, the God who is our salvation. God is to us a God of deliverances" (Psalm 68:19-20 NASB).

3. Take a long, hard look at yourself. God gives no blessing to Christians who hold out on Him. "If I regard wickedness in my heart, the Lord will not hear" (Psalm 66:18 NASB). If we want our minds renewed, we must be painfully honest—both with God and ourselves. Search out and confess those thoughts that displease Him.

4. Make a 100 percent commitment. There must come a point at which we are revolted at our own vileness. It is at this point that God wants the Christian to resolve to "go all the way with God's way." This means conforming every thought to the holiness enjoined in Scripture. David put it this way: "Your word is a lamp to my feet and a light for my path . . . I will follow your righteous laws . . . My heart is set on keeping your decrees to the very end" (Psalm 119:105–106, 112 NIV).

5. Be flexible and willing to change. Jesus likened a stagnant Christian to an old wineskin—no longer flexible, incapable of holding new wine. Christians who have become narrow-minded, stale, and complacent are especially vulnerable to ungodly thoughts. These we must set aside. God's goal for us is the perfect holiness exemplified in His Son.

6. See God as the only refuge. We live in a society geared toward human pride and self-sufficiency. Even Christians sometimes forget that only God is our true deliverer. David acknowledged as much, saying, "The help of man is worthless . . ." (Psalm 60:11 NIV), and "Pour out your heart before Him; God is our refuge" (Psalm 62:8).

7. Renewal is a full-time job. Romans 12:2 teaches that we are "transformed by the renewing of [our] mind[s]." But we must be vigilant. A daily quiet time in the Word is essential. Are you often troubled by an unclean thought? Find the appropriate Scripture and quote it to yourself when that thought comes around again. Start memorizing Scripture—maybe three or four verses every week. Learn to meditate on Scripture, asking the Holy Spirit for aid and illumination. Ask God to reveal His attributes to you. Seek to know Him in every thought and deed.

Follow through on these seven guidelines, and you will find your thinking more and more Christlike. Much is at stake here. You can choose to cleanse your mind with God's Holy Word, or surrender it to unclean thoughts prompted by Satan, God's adversary and ours.

YOU CAN WIN THE VICTORY

First Corinthians 10 opens by reminding us how the Israelites were tempted in the wilderness. God was not pleased with them, and they were "scattered over the desert" (verse 5 NIV). The apostle Paul then goes on to tell us that these things happened for our example (verses 6–11).

The first step in conquering temptation is to face our sin and its terrible consequences. All too often, we try to rationalize away the seriousness of sin and thereby fall victim to its clutches. Sin is no laughing matter with God. It is rebellious disobedience to His law. If we will follow God's prescription for conquering temptation, we can keep ourselves from falling into sin.

1. Admit to yourself that you are being tempted. Acknowledge your feelings. Face your temptation head-on and determine to *do* something about it!

2. Confess to God that you are tempted to sin. We are not only to confess our sins to God, but even the very fact that we *desire* to sin. Remember that God sees everything you are doing, and He knows everything you are thinking (see Psalm 139:2). Run to Him in prayer and ask for His help now, before you sin.

3. Seek the help of a Christian friend. Two kinds of friends are to be avoided: the harsh, censorious type and the overlenient type. Go to someone who will help you turn from sin without turning from you. Ask to pray with that person. The Bible reminds us that we are to "carry each other's burdens" (Galatians 6:2 NIV).

4. There are no excuses for failure. The Bible promises, "No temptation has seized you except what is common to man" (1 Corinthians 10:13 NIV). Others have won out over temptation; why should you be an exception? Sin is sin. Stop thinking about what to do or why you are feeling overwhelmed, and decide to do what you know is right! "Resist the devil and he will flee from you" (James 4:7).

5. Trust God to give you the victory. He is faithful! If you really believe that, you will deal with your temptation by making "no provision for the flesh." You cannot expect God to help you when, at the same time, you are preparing to disobey Him.

6. Take the "way of escape"! Get away from the source of your temptation. Don't try to get as close as you can to temptation. Get as far away from it as possible!

The battle for the heart is an extension of the spiritual warfare of our times. The same tempter who suggested to Eve that God didn't know what He was talking about is up to his old tricks today. By appealing to the desire of the heart, Satan bypasses our mental processes. Our capacity for logical reasoning is blinded by the desires of the heart. Before we know it, we are lured into choices we never dreamed we would make.

The constant bombardment of television shows, advertising commercials, music, movies, videos, and the Internet keeps telling us that it is "normal" to indulge ourselves in the sensual pleasures of life. There are few, if any, warnings about the consequences of such indulgence. Our society cries out for freedom of expression for the most grotesque and sinful lifestyles and then wonders why we have such a high divorce rate, angry children, and hurting families. We cannot have it both ways. We must either live by God's standards or by the world's values.

There is a moral and spiritual sickness permeating every area of our national existence. Every year brings some hideous new expression of blatant disregard for God's laws. As human behavior slouches toward moral oblivion, our society continues to disintegrate. The moral fiber has eroded from the fabric of the postmodern world. We are a sick society. But like all other addicts, we keep insisting that we can handle this. We keep telling ourselves that it's really not that bad. We're really not that bad.

We want to believe that we could yet turn back from the brink of moral and social disaster. But the truth is, we have already gone over the edge! We are in a spiritual free fall that could well lead to the end of Western civilization. We need help, and we need it now!

3

The Death
of the Soul

Therefore we do not lose heart.
—*2 CORINTHIANS 4:16*

DURING THE EARLY DAYS OF ADOLF HITLER'S rise to power in Germany, he invited a number of pastors and community leaders to a personal meeting with their new leader. As he laid out his vision for a new Germany, only one young pastor objected.

"What about the soul of Germany?" the pastor asked.

"You take care of your church," Hitler snapped, "and leave the soul of Germany to me!"[1]

Unfortunately, that is exactly what most church people in Germany did. They went about their normal religious duties and rituals while der Führer stole the hearts of the Germans and corrupted the soul of the nation. By the end of World War II, the soul of Germany and much of the rest of Europe was spiritually dead.

In the blockbuster bestseller *Care of the Soul,* Thomas Moore's opening sentence said it all. He wrote, "The greatest malady of the twentieth century, implicated in all our troubles and affecting us individually and socially, is *loss of soul.*[2] When the soul is neglected, Moore suggested, we experience obsessions, addictions, violence, loss of meaning, and emotional pain. Calling himself an "anti-self-help advocate," Moore separates himself from the views of pop psychology, but his perspectives on the "soul" express the spiritual hunger of our times.

Our generation is painfully aware that something is missing in their lives. They are turning to books, tapes, videos, gurus, mystical experiences, and a host of self-focused attempts at spirituality. They can't face the ultimate conclusions of rationalism—that there is no God and we are alone in a meaningless universe. A century and a half of this kind of thinking has drained the spiritual life out of Western civilization.

We cannot remain blinded to the seriousness of this situation. Nor can we remain neutral in the battle for the heart and mind—individually and collectively. People are "losing heart" personally, and in many cases, the church has lost heart as well. We have retreated to our cloistered congregations and isolated ourselves from a world that is spiritually dying.

Unless we face the enormity of this task, we will lose every belief that we hold dear and the institutions that are extensions of those beliefs—home, church, and state. We must be willing to capture every idea of our age and bring each one under the Lordship of Christ or those ideas will capture us. Our hearts, souls, and minds are at stake—even our very lives.

THE ATTACK ON THE SOUL

The human soul, like the human heart, is the expression of the inner life of the human existence. It is the area within us where our God-consciousness is inflamed by the Spirit of God. It is in our inner selves that we intuitively sense that we are made for communion with God. Theologians call this God-awareness the *imago dei* (image of God). It is that aspect of God's creative genius that enables us to know Him, despite our fallen nature.

The image of God was effaced by sin, but not erased. It was distorted, but not eliminated. There is left in every human heart the realization that there is Someone greater than ourselves. Theologians, philosophers, and psychologists call this the "mystery of transcendence." It is that inner sense that the real meaning of life transcends our mere physical existence. But this awareness alone is not enough to lead us to a personal relationship with God—that is only revealed to us in the divinely inspired Scriptures.

As the twentieth century drew to a close, it became painfully obvious that our generation had not only lost confidence in the Bible but in God Himself. The century-long bombardment of secular humanism had taken its toll on the soul of America in the twentieth century just as it had in Europe in the nineteenth century. Once a society loses its heart and soul, it loses all sense of the transcendence of the divine, and life becomes little more than a meaningless existence.

Brent Curtis and John Eldredge express it like this: "To lose heart is to lose everything. And a 'loss of heart' best describes most men and women in our day. It isn't just the addictions and affairs and depression and heartaches, though God knows, there are enough of these to cause even the best of us to lose heart. But there is the busyness, the drivenness, the fact that most of us are living merely to survive. Beneath it we feel restless, weary and vulnerable."[3]

The impact of the anti-God bias of secular education has left our generation without God, morality, meaning, or purpose. We are a society adrift on a sea of moral relativism that can only be described as "lost." This theme of cultural emptiness and personal lost hearts, which is nothing more than an expression of the emptiness of the human soul, dominates today's music and entertainment.

Even in religious circles, there is a growing tendency to view God as someone who exists to meet our needs. Psychologist Dr. Larry Crabb writes, "We Christians cannot talk about loving God until we come to grips with our raging passion for ourselves. We can not and will not love anyone but ourselves until we meet God in a way that stirs us to race after him with single-minded intensity, until our deepest desire is to get to know him better."[4] He summarizes his appeal by adding: "I must surrender my fascination with myself to a more worthy preoccupation with the character and purposes of God. I am not the point. He is."[5]

THE DIRECT PATH TO DESTRUCTION

Satan's schemes are not obvious. Otherwise they would not be schemes, and they would certainly not work as well as they do. And while we must never blame the devil in an attempt to shirk responsibility, we can be wise to his ways.

One simple way to remember how our enemy leads us from compromise to compromise is by remembering the *D* words—starting with the *devil* himself. After that, the pattern of how you will feel and what will happen to you looks something like this:

1. Devoted. This is where we want to be, every step along the path of righteousness. Devoted to God, to the gifts He's given us, and to the work He's called us to. Devoted to our relationships and to doing right. But detour signs await us at every turn, and if we're not careful we'll step onto a different, darker path. In no time at all we'll arrive at the first signpost and find that something is different.

2. Distracted. Instead of spending time with the Lord, this stage finds you too busy. You are not involved in bad activities at this point, simply too occupied for prayer and Bible study. Too overloaded for Christian fellowship and eventually even Sunday service.

3. Discontent. This stage is marked by a restless feeling, an inner longing in your heart that tells you something is missing.

4. Discouraged. Stay discontent long enough and you will find yourself at this point on the path. Everything is hard now. Your job, your dreams, your relationships. The heart cries out for some new and different way to satisfy its hunger.

5. Deceived. This happens the moment you commit your first true compromise. Not the little bad choices—the forgotten Bible and forgotten birthday dinner—but the type of decisions that once would have been blatantly forbidden. Deception sneaks around in soft shoes and leads you to a place of justification. "I deserve the affair . . ." "No one will notice the missing money . . ." "It'll never happen again." The excuse list is long and in time leads directly to the next stop along the path.

6. Denial. When sin is given free reign, the devil will do his best to keep you in denial. This is the place where our bodies go about one set of activities, while our minds are someplace altogether different. We tell ourselves we'll stop, we'll start fresh, we'll walk away. But almost always, denial leaves us feeling one way.

7. Devastated. When the consequences of our actions are first obvious, nearly everyone will feel some degree of devastation. Your life will seem irreversibly harmed by your season of bad choices, and these feelings of hopelessness lead to one of two choices. Some people may repent and seek God; others will feel too far gone to turn back. For them, the final destination is right around the corner.

8. Destroyed. The end of the wrong path is sad, indeed. A person who is destroyed will likely lose everything that once mattered. His family, his job, his home, his faith. Even his life. And certainly for those who never found Christ, never accepted His free gift of forgiveness, the ultimate destination is eternal death. The last *D* word on the path to destruction.

THE EMPTINESS OF OUR TIMES

Twenty centuries ago, the apostle Paul looked down the corridor of time and foresaw what he called "terrible times." He put it like this: "But mark this: There will be terrible times in the last days. People will be lovers of themselves, lovers of money, boastful, proud, abusive, disobedient to their parents, ungrateful, unholy, without love, unforgiving, slanderous, without self-control, brutal, not lovers of the good, treacherous, rash, conceited, lovers of pleasure, rather than lovers of God (2 Timothy 3:1–4 NIV).

The apostle's prophetic analysis is an apt description of our times. Ours is a culture absorbed with itself. We have little interest in the values and principles that made us great. Instead, we exalt the vices that are destined to destroy us. The battle for the mind parallels the battle for the heart. Once we surrender our Christian beliefs to the secularism of our age, we leave our hearts vulnerable to Satan's attacks on every area of our lives.[6]

These battles for the minds and hearts of Americans are really a single battle for the soul of our nation. This great conflict between the intellectual and spiritual forces of good and evil has come in five distinct waves. Each one has prepared for the next in such a way that our Christian-based culture has been inundated by a tidal wave so destructive that it has left little of our spiritual heritage intact.

1. Secularism. The first wave of attack on the foundations of our Judeo-Christian heritage has been the wave of secularism. Most of our schools and our public educational systems have been totally engulfed in the rising tide of humanistic and secular beliefs that eliminate God from any relevance to our culture. Today, we have kids without convictions because our adult generation has sacrificed them on the altars of intellectualism. They have been taught there is no God, life is an accident of biological chance, and there is no real meaning to our existence. It is no wonder that teen suicides are at an all-time high. It should not surprise us that school shootings are out of control or that teenage pregnancies are at record levels. Secularism has poisoned the intellectual minds of today's generation.

2. Relativism. Relativism follows quickly on the heels of secularism. It is the belief that all truth is relative to its context. It is the end result of a rationalism that loses it rationality. Once we reason that belief in God is not a rational option, we open our souls to believing in the irrational. Attempting to be wise, we become fools. We create our own agendas for life. Relativism basically tells us, "If it feels good, do it!" Absolutes of truth and morality are swept aside in favor of a new philosophy of life that exalts self-gratification and eliminates all absolute standards of human behavior.

3. Selfism. The driving force at the center of this current intellectual, moral, and emotional revisionism is our pre-occupation with ourselves. We have become the measure of all things. We have no real concern for truth, justice, or integrity, except as they relate to us. We want everyone else to be held to some moral standard, but we don't want to apply that standard to ourselves. We prefer to exalt ourselves above such standards. The rules are for others to go by, but not us. We have become a law unto ourselves. "Me," "myself," and "I" have become the center of our own personal universes.

4. Materialism. Ironically, most people really can't stand themselves. So they quickly shift their focus from self-preoccupation to materialistic gratification. We fill our lives with *things* in the hope that those things will make us happy. But, alas, they too disappoint us. Our new cars soon become used cars. Our new jobs take on demands and pressures of their own that sap the joy out of living. The more we have, the more we want. In time, nothing satisfies us. We find ourselves grasping after the "toys" of life in the hope that something will make us happy. Our consumer indulgence drives us to crave for every new gadget and device that technology can provide. But we are left, in the end, with a pile of "stuff" we don't really need or want.

5. Mysticism. When the things of life do not make us happy, we turn to experiences to find worth and meaning to our existence. This is where our culture is today. We have allowed the forces of secularism to rob our hearts of the real meaning of life. Our minds have closed to the truth, and our souls have turned to the ridiculous to find a replacement for our need for God. In the place of the God of the Bible, our culture has turned to demonism, Satanism, witchcraft, tea leaves, tarot cards, mediums, seances, and crystals. Reincarnation has replaced regeneration in today's mystical theology. The "spirits" have replaced the Holy Spirit. Jesus is viewed as an exalted human, not a divine Savior.

A generation ago, such a love affair with mystical experiences would have been scorned by the rationalistic minds of human secularism. But today, these ideas are readily accepted as legitimate self-expressions of the human need for transcendence. Our secular society has come to the end of its intellectual rope and lost its mind!

THE MORTICIANS ARE HERE!

The death of Western culture is a fact that is well established both by secular and religious thinkers.[7] The patient is dead. The heart has stopped beating. The morticians are in the lobby. Still, the doctors of the soul are scurrying about to see if there are any other options left. Resuscitation? Electropulmonary shock? In the meantime, the life-support systems have been hooked up to artificially sustain the victim.

The diagnosis is serious. The patient is in trouble. Some would advocate letting her die. Others want to go on pretending that she will recover. Still others suggest leaving her on life support. They would encourage us to continue our recovery efforts, knowing that they will do very little to revive the patient. This latter group would continue to go on with their normal spiritual routines hoping that their freedom to do so will not be affected by the patient's death. These are those who are content for their faith to remain irrelevant in the public domain of society. They are satisfied that their religious experience meets their own personal needs, but they have no real compulsion to share it with anyone else.

There is another model for dealing with the patient. It is much more drastic. The risks are greater. But so are the prospects for recovery.

The patient needs a heart transplant.

The Bible refers to this as having a "new heart." This is a process of spiritual regeneration and transformation that only God can produce.

Matters of the heart are God's chief concern. God promised that He would give His people a new heart and a new spirit. He said, "I will give you a new heart and put a new spirit in you; I will remove from you your heart of stone and give you a heart of flesh. And I will put my Spirit in you and move you to follow my decrees and be careful to keep my laws" (Ezekiel 36:26–27 NIV).

God promises that we can experience a radical transformation of heart and spirit. This is a fundamental change that occurs from within and is produced by God. It is not the result of self-improvement or human effort. It is the work of divine intervention into our helpless situation. The Bible also reminds us, "The heart is deceitful above all things, and desperately wicked" (Jeremiah 17:9). Our entire being has been permeated and corrupted by sin, and we are powerless to change it.

But God is a heart surgeon of incomparable skill. He removes our old, dead hearts of stone and replaces them with living hearts that are responsive to Him. These new hearts provide us with new life, new direction, new desires, and new possibilities.

God also promises to put His Spirit in us. In the Old Testament the Spirit came *on* people but did not live *in* people. The promise of God's indwelling Spirit must have sounded strange to the prophet's listeners. Much later Jesus promised that the Holy Spirit would reside both *on* and *in* believers (John 16:5–15). When we receive Jesus Christ by faith, the Spirit of God enters our lives and infuses us with power to live for God.

Jesus made it clear that we are incapable of camouflaging that which lies deepest within our hearts. He said, "Where your treasure is, there your heart will be also" (Matthew 6:21). Later, He added, "Out of the abundance of the heart the mouth speaks" (Matthew 12:34).

The bottom line of Jesus' teaching was that the spiritual life is a matter of the heart. Summarizing the Old Testament Law, Jesus affirmed, "Love the Lord your God with all your heart, with all your soul, with all your mind, and with all your strength" (Mark 12:30). With heart, soul, mind, and strength—in other words, with everything—we are called to love our God. And out of this love will inevitably flow an outpouring of heartfelt love and service to God.

This is what the world needs, but insists it can do without. We need a doctor of the heart and soul who can transform our inner being. Without that divine surgeon, we are destined to a slow and painful death. The corpse of Western civilization is getting colder every day. Without divine intervention, it will not resurrect itself.

The Bible urges us, "Do not lose heart" (2 Corinthians 4:16). Despite the bleak prospects of the future of a world without God, we hold fast to God's promises for the last days. There are two parallel, yet opposite, streams of biblical prophecies about the future. On the one hand, the Bible promises the spread of the gospel and the growth of the church until Jesus comes (see Matthew 16:18 and 24:14).

On the other hand, it also predicts the increase of wickedness and the spread of evil as we near the end of the age (see Matthew 24:12; 2 Timothy 3:1–5).

Both streams of biblical prophecy are equally true. We have a mandate to proclaim the gospel of Jesus Christ no matter how evil the days may become. But we do so with the solemn awareness that this world is inevitably on a collision course with disaster. Unless we experience a genuine revival of biblical spirituality and righteousness, there is no real hope for the future. We can call for the divine doctor or bring in the morticians. The choice is ours.

4

Is There a
Doctor in the House?

It is not the healthy who need a doctor, but the sick.
—MATTHEW 9:12 NIV

JIM AIMED HIS GUN AT THE POLICE OFFICER'S head and placed his finger on the trigger. A circle of policemen around him closed in.

"It isn't worth it!" one of them shouted.

"Drop it. Come on. You don't want to do this . . ." An officer inched closer.

Fifteen tense seconds passed and slowly, with tears in his eyes, Jim dropped the gun to the ground. "Okay." The college student began to sob. "I'm sorry. I . . . I was so upset, I wanted to shoot someone. But I couldn't do it."

Jim was a college student. He was having a bad year academically, and he had just broken up with his girlfriend. Seeing her with another guy the next day pushed him over the edge. He threatened to shoot them both but stopped just as police arrived.

"It was like I was in a movie." He explained what happened later at the police station. "I grabbed the gun and started threatening them. I never planned to hurt anyone."

Jim is like a lot of young people today. They don't know what motivated their behavior—whether it's the clothes they buy or the threats they make. Our entire generation seems detached from reality. We have forgotten who we are. It seems as though we are watching a portrayal of our lives on a screen.

Twenty years ago, the remote Gwinchin tribe in Alaska got television for the first time. Satellite dishes, video games, and VCRs followed. For the first time in their tribal existence, their old ways of hunting, language, family, and oral history began to disappear. Their cultural heritage was replaced by younger tribe members who were drawn to television. Moccasins gave way to sneakers, dog sleds to skimobiles, and tundra tea to instant coffee. Soon, teenage violence followed.

Jean Kilbourne tells the story of this tribe's cultural conversion in her compelling book, *Deadly Persuasion*.[1] What happened to the Gwinchins in less than twenty years is what is happening to our culture as well. Our basic beliefs, values, and lifestyles are being replaced by the virtual reality of media bombardment of the heart and soul of America. Programmers and advertisers alike are bypassing the critical aspects of human reasoning by appealing to our emotions in order to get us to accept their messages. Don't think—just do it! An advertising slogan has become a national lifestyle. "Follow your heart" has replaced "Watch your step."

The visual impact of media on American life has been going on for over half a century now. But factual studies analyzing this impact have been few and far between. It is almost as though we are reluctant to tell ourselves the truth about our deadly addiction with our electronic suitor. In the past few years, however, several legitimate studies have been done by reputable researchers that verify the devastating effects of media on the soul of America.

Today's young people are the most media-savvy generation in history. They have every kind of electronic gadget imaginable. But they are not happy. Most are struggling to discover meaning and purpose in their lives. They often see themselves as victims of a broken world, and far too many are suffering from the impact of divorce, rejection, and abandonment. Some view their electronic companions as their only true "friends." Others are simply trapped by technology. They live their lives in an impersonal world of screens, wires, and projected images.

This wave of cool indifference has resulted from our national love affair with technology and has deadened our hearts, nullified our spirits, and corrupted our souls. It has left a whole generation wondering who they are and why they are here. The time has come for us to be honest with ourselves about what is fundamentally wrong with our culture. We have abandoned truth for experience. We have replaced God with greed. We have lost our minds in a world of extrasensual experiences, overstimulated senses, and underdeveloped values. We are caught in the sticky web of virtual reality and have lost all consciousness of right and wrong.

Satan is winning the battle for the heart because he is an expert at using the media to appeal to our emotions, bypass our consciences, and corrupt our minds. It is for this very reason that we need to understand how this process works.

INFLUENCE OF MEDIA ON THE MIND

Dr. Robert Sylvester, professor of education at the University of Oregon, is one of America's leading researchers on how human emotions affect learning.[2] He points out:

> Emotion drives attention, which drives learning, memory, and behavior, so mass media often insert strong primal emotional elements into their programming to

increase attention. Since violence and sexuality in media trigger primal emotions, most young people confront thousands of violent acts and heavy doses of sexuality during their childhood media interactions. This comes at the expense, alas, of other more positive and normative experiences with human behaviors and interactions. Mass media tend to show us how to be sexy not sexual, and powerful not peaceful.

Commercial sponsorship in mass media has led to a distorted presentation of important cultural and consumer-related issues. For example, TV commercials tend to be very short, superficial, and factually biased. Further, computer programs and TV editing techniques tend to compress, extend, and distort normal time/space relationships, a critically important element in the creation and use of effective long-term memories.[3]

Our brain uses two systems to analyze and respond to environmental challenges, and electronic mass media often exploit these systems:

1. A relatively **slow, analytic, reflective** system (thalamus-hippocampus-cortex circuitry) explores the more objective factual elements of a situation, compares them with related declarative memories, and then responds. It's best suited to nonthreatening situations that don't require an instant response—life's little challenges.

2. A **fast conceptual, reflexive** system (thalamus-amygdala-cerebellum circuitry) identifies the fearful and survival elements in a situation, and quickly activates automatic response patterns (procedural memory) if survival seems problematic.

The fast system developed through natural selection to respond to imminent predatory danger and feeding and mating opportunities. It thus focuses on any elements that might signal potential danger, food, and/or mates.

The system thus enhances survival, but its rapid superficial analysis often leads us to respond fearfully, impulsively, and inappropriately to situations that didn't require an immediate response. (Regrets and apologies often follow.) Worse, fear can strengthen the emotional and weaken the factual memories of an event.

People often use mass media to exploit this system by stressing elements that trigger rapid irrational fear responses. Politicians demonize opponents; sales pitches demand an immediate response; zealots focus on fear of groups who differ from their definition of acceptable.

The fast pacing of TV and video game programming, and their focus on bizarre/violent/sexual elements also trigger this system. If the audience perceives these elements and the resulting visceral responses as the real-world norm, the electronic media must continually escalate the violent/sexual/bizarre behavior to trigger the fast system. Rational thought development would thus suffer.[4]

George Gerbner, one of the world's most respected researchers on the influence of the media, says, "For the first time in human history, most of the stories about people, life, and values are not told by parents, schools, churches, or others in the community who have something to tell, but by a group of distant conglomerates that have something to sell."[5]

In our contemporary culture the media have become the key to our social identity. We are shaped by the media we watch. Marshall McLuhan has said, "The medium is the message!"[6] American jurist Learned Hand put it more bluntly: "The art of publicity is a black art."[7] British author Malcolm Muggeridge wrote, "History will see advertising as one of the real evils of our time."[8] Psychologist Eric Fromm pointed out, "A vast sector of modern advertising does not appeal to reason but to emotion; like any other kind of hypnoid suggestion, it tries to impress its objects emotionally and then make them submit intellectually."[9]

Most national advertising includes the embedding of hidden stimuli that appeal to our emotions while bypassing our brains. Material, social, and sexual images drive the advertising on television with a constant bombardment of the human conscience, stripping away our beliefs and values and leaving us prey to the whims of the advertisers. It invades the judgment of children, forces its way into the family, and usurps parental functions.

If advertising can affect human behavior, so can television and movies. They appeal to our emotions and tell us what to believe about ourselves and others. The Center for Media Literacy in Los Angeles emphasizes the five core concepts about media:

1. All media productions are constructions. Media are carefully manufactured cultural products. They create an emotional experience that looks like reality. Media are not "real" but they affect people in real ways because we interpret meaning by what we see, hear and read.

2. Media productions use unique languages. Media Language is unique to each form of communication. The language is used over and over as a shorthand for conveying intended meanings.

3. Audiences negotiate meaning. No two people see the same movie or hear the same song. We may not be conscious of it, but we are constantly trying to make sense out of what we see, hear or read.

4. Media productions have commercial interests. Media productions are ad-driven businesses. Corporate sponsors pay the bills. Advertisers want specific kinds of viewers who are likely to buy their products.

5. Media productions have embedded values. Media, by their very nature, carry a subtext of who and what is important. There are no value-free media. This means each of us must learn to "read" the media critically as we negotiate our way through our mediated environment.[10]

Most of us have watched enough media to realize that we are constantly being "sold" something. What we often don't understand is that we are being sold ideas, beliefs, and values—not just products. The subtlety of these ideas is such that we can find ourselves cheering for a hero with questionable morals just because he or she is depicted in the media as a hero, rather than a villain. It is the ideologies of the producers and writers that determine the values and beliefs that are taught by appealing to the emotions.

EFFECTS OF MEDIA ON THE FAMILY

One of the most revealing studies of the impact of television violence was conducted by the Center for Communication and Social Policy at the University of California at Santa Barbara.[11] The facts they uncovered clearly demonstrate the impact of media influence on the American family.

- In 1950, only 10 percent of American homes had a television and by 1960 the percentage had grown to 90 percent. Today 99 percent of homes have a television. In fact, more families own a television than a phone.

- Fifty-four percent of U.S. children have a television set in their bedrooms.

- Children spend more time learning about life through media than in any other manner. The average child spends approximately twenty eight hours a week watching television, which is twice as much time as they spend in school.

- The average American child will witness over 200,000 acts of violence on television including 16,000 murders before age eighteen.

- Polls further show that three-quarters of the public find television entertainment too violent. When asked to select measures that would reduce violent crime "a lot," Americans chose restrictions on television violence more often than gun control.

- A study of population data for various countries showed homicide rates doubling within the ten to fifteen years after the introduction of television, even though television was introduced at different times in each site examined.

- Longitudinal studies tracking viewing habits and behavior patterns of a single individual found that eight-year-old boys, who viewed the most violent programs growing up, were the most likely to engage in aggressive and delinquent behavior by age eighteen and serious criminal behavior by age thirty.

• Watching TV has been linked to obesity in children.

• Studies suggest that higher rates of television viewing are correlated with increased tobacco usage, increased alcohol intake, and younger onset of sexual activity.

• Potential adverse effects of excessive exposure to media include increased violent behavior; obesity, decreased physical activity and fitness, increased cholesterol levels and sodium intake; repetitive strain injury (video computer games); insomnia; photic seizures; impaired school performance; increased sexual activity and use of tobacco and alcohol; decreased attention span; decreased family communication; desensitization; excess consumer focus.

• Fifty-five percent of children questioned usually watch television alone or with a friend, but not with their families.

• According to the National Television Violence Study, the context in which violence is portrayed is as important to its impact as the amount of violence. The study concluded that 66 percent of children's programming had violence. Of the shows with violent content, three-quarters demonstrated unpunished violence and when violence occurred, 58 percent of the time victims were not shown experiencing pain.

• Forty-six percent of all television violence identified by the study took place in children's cartoons. Children's programs were least likely to depict the long-term consequences of violence (5 percent) and they portray violence in a humorous fashion 67 percent of the time.

• The use of parental warnings and violence advisories made the programs more of a magnet than they might otherwise have been. Parental Discretion Advised and PG-13 and R ratings significantly increased boys' interest in the shows, although they made girls less interested in watching.

A similar study done by Canadian researcher Arlene Moscovitch of the Vanier Institute of the Family indicates that television viewing is becoming more of an individual activity, with two or three TV sets in a household, and less of a communal family activity. Moscovitch observes, "Even a cursory glance shows that media experiences have become an integral part of the weave of everyday life. In fact, it's difficult to think of an area not included in the media embrace. In both the public and private sphere, we consume and (some would say) are consumed by a flood of images and sounds which carry insistent and powerful messages."[12]

Canadian professor Stephen Kline of Simon Fraser University in British Columbia studied the video gaming habits of young people, aged eleven to eighteen. He found that

- Video games have been incorporated into the daily routines of 65 percent of all Canadian households, including 85 percent with male children.

- 25 percent of the young people surveyed considered themselves addicted and admitted they were troubled about their compulsive behavior.

- Canadian Internet users spend about eight hours per week on-line.

- Parents pay little or no attention to what their children play on the Internet.[13]

British studies indicate that 83 percent of thirteen- and fourteen-year-olds have a television in their bedrooms, compared to 50 percent in the United States.[14] About half of all children in Britain and the U.S. watch television alone or with friends, but not with parents. Moscovitch believes this trend greatly diminishes the significance of viewer-rating systems if there are no parents around to monitor their children's television viewing or Internet usage. She observes, "As more time is spent in solitary watching, there's less time for family conversation, less interaction around other forms of indoor recreation and less opportunity for children to learn 'doing' skills from their parents, or other family members."[15]

Television and Internet video games have become America's electronic babysitters. The Internet is growing faster than all other preceding media technologies. It took radio thirty-eight years before it had fifty million listeners. Television took thirteen years to reach that mark. But it only took four years for the Internet to top fifty million users. Now, the introduction of Web TV, which marries television and the Internet, has the potential to become the most powerful media influence in the world.

Fr. John Pungente of the Jesuit Communications Project in Toronto states, "By the time the average North American child graduates from high school, he or she will have:

- Spent 11,000 hours in the classroom.

- Watched 15,000 hours of television.

- Seen 350,000 commercials.

- Watched 40,000 violent deaths.

- Listened to 10,500 hours of pop music.

- Gone to 400 movies.[16]

Arlene Moscovitch adds, "Through these media interactions, children are exposed to a staggering amount of
entertainment and information about how the world
works, and what it is that makes life worth living. They
learn a lot from this 'informal curriculum' about heroes and
villains and victims, about being male and female, about
how to achieve success in life, about who's got power and
who doesn't, about violence and intimate relations and
what constitutes the 'good life.'"[17]

IMPACT OF MEDIA VIOLENCE

The psychological problem with media violence is that it
blurs the lines between image and reality. Today, media violence is depicted with such shocking reality that it is just
like being there in person—heads explode, blood splatters,
and limbs are dismembered. But an even greater problem is
created by the fact that the viewer experiences no pain or
consequences.

George Gerbner, Dean Emeritus of the Annenberg
School of Communications and a pioneer in the study of
media violence notes:

- According to the *Unesco Global Study on Media Violence*, the impact of media violence is so great primarily
  because aggressive behavior is rewarded.

- The National Television Violence Study, funded by the U.S. cable industry, analyzed the context in which violence was depicted and found that perpetrators of violent acts on television go unpunished 73 percent of the time. Bad characters are punished 62 percent of the time, good characters only 15 percent of the time. Forty-seven percent of all violent interactions showed no resulting harm to the victims, and 58 percent depicted no pain. Longer-term consequences, such as financial or emotional harm, were shown only 16 percent of the time.

- Twenty-five percent of all violent acts on television involve the use of a handgun. Only four percent of programs containing violence emphasized non-violent alternatives to solving problems.

- Children's programs posed special concerns because they were least likely to depict the long-term consequences of violence (five percent) and they portray violence in a humorous fashion 67% of the time.[18]

The "Joint Statement on the Impact of Entertainment Violence on Children" points out that, while entertainment media can instruct, encourage, and inspire, "when these entertainment media showcase violence—and particularly in a context which glamorizes or trivializes it—the lessons learned can be destructive."[19] This is especially true because prolonged viewing of media violence can lead to emotional desensitization toward violence in real life. The "Joint Statement," sponsored by the American Academy of Pediatrics, American Psychological Association, American Medical Association, and the American Academy of Child and Adolescent Psychiatry, points out:

> There are some in the entertainment industry who maintain that 1) violent programming is harmless because no studies exist that prove a connection between violent entertainment and aggressive behavior in children, and 2) young people know that television, movies, and video games are simply fantasy. Unfortunately, they are wrong on both counts.
>
> At this time, well over 1000 studies—including reports from the Surgeon General's office, the National Institute of Mental Health, and numerous studies conducted by leading figures within our medical and public health organizations—our own members—point overwhelmingly to a causal connection between media violence and aggressive behavior in some children. The conclusion of the public health community, based on over 30 years of research, is that viewing entertainment violence can lead to increases in aggressive attitudes, values and behavior, particularly in children.[20]

They concluded that there are several measurable effects of children's exposure to violent entertainment. These include

- Children who see a lot of violence are more likely to view violence as an effective way of settling conflicts. Children exposed to violence are more likely to assume that acts of violence are acceptable behavior.

- Viewing violence can lead to emotional desensitization toward violence in real life. It can decrease the likelihood that one will take action on behalf of a victim when violence occurs.

- Entertainment violence feeds a perception that the world is a violent and mean place. Viewing violence increases fear of becoming a victim of violence, with a resultant increase in self-protective behaviors and a mistrust of others.

- Viewing violence may lead to real-life violence. Children exposed to violent programming at a young age have a higher tendency for violent and aggressive behavior later in life than children who are not so exposed.[21]

In December 1997, fifteen-year-old Michael Carneal opened fire on his classmates at Heath High School in West Paducah, Kentucky, killing three of them. After the shooting, Carneal told investigators that he had seen his crime portrayed in the film *The Basketball Diaries*, in which the lead character, played by Leonardo DiCaprio, dreams of shooting up a school. Carneal said that he felt he was in a dream when he fired on a group of students who had just finished an informal prayer session in the hallway. The movie, based on the life of writer Jim Carroll, contains several negative portrayals of religion.

The terrible legacy of school shootings is now at epidemic proportions in America's public schools. When disaffected kids like Columbine's Eric Harris and Dylan Klebold stockpile guns and homemade bombs, it is obvious that something is wrong with the hearts of young people in our secularized society. Recent shootings in California at Santee and Granite Hills in El Cajon, near where I (Tim) used to minister as a pastor, have broken the hearts of young people and parents alike. Something is wrong with this generation, and everyone knows it!

There are many contributing factors—rising divorce rates, broken homes, fatherless families, media and video-game violence, and angry music may all be contributing factors. But the deeper problem is the darkness of the human heart. "The anxieties and angers that used to be free-floating in adolescents now simply attach themselves to events like Columbine," says University of California at Berkeley law professor Franklin Zimring. "Instead of just talking about it, now they have a model."[22]

"It's only me," Andy Williams said as he surrendered his gun in the boy's rest room at the high school in Santee, California, having shot several people. Unfortunately, school violence is not limited to one person. The list is endless—Lake Worth, Florida; Fort Gibson, Oklahoma; Deming, New Mexico. Each of these incidents is an expression of the empty-heartedness of our society, which is spawning a culture of cruelty.

Retired Lt. Col. David Grossman, former professor of psychology at West Point, who presently teaches a course on the psychology of killing to the Green Berets, appeared on the CBS television show *60 Minutes* on April 25, 1999. Grossman referred to violent video games as "murder simulators." He told interviewers, "The average child in America spends countless hundreds of hours practicing and practicing on murder simulators. And when some of them go out and execute it, we should not be surprised."[23] Grossman warned that violent video games enable kids to turn their fantasies into reality. When asked why he believed this, Grossman added, "It teaches you to associate pleasure with human death and suffering. Until we stop this, the killings won't stop!"

In a hearing before the Senate Commerce Committee, Debbie Pelley, a teacher at Westside Middle School in Jonesboro, Arkansas, testified that thirteen-year-old Mitchell Johnson, involved in killing four students and one teacher and injuring ten others, was addicted to the gangster rap music of 2 Pac Shakur. She said, "Mitchell brought the music to school with him, listened to it on the bus, tried listening to it in classes, sang the lyrics over and over at school, and played a cassette in the bathroom 'about coming to school and killing all the kids.'"[24]

Dr. Robert Sylvester writes, "The attentional demands of electronic media range from rapt (video games) to passive (Mach TV), but this is the first generation to directly interact with and alter the content on the screen and the conversation on the radio. Screenagers emotionally understand electronic media in ways that adults don't—a virtual replacing cultural reality, instead of a mere communicator of events."[25]

The only way to avoid the adverse effects of violence in the media is when the individual viewer disassociates visual stimuli as an aberration of reality (as do most adults). But children who grow up in a nonsecure environment tend to react to such electronic experiences as though they are both real and desirable. Rapid irrational responses trigger violent actions as an expression of one's inner fears and frustrations. The result is school violence on an unprecedented scale.

The bombardment of the hearts of our nation's young people by the media is reaping terrible consequences. Their young minds and responsive hearts cannot endure the constant impact of television, movies, videos, and music that are designed to rob the human soul of its spiritual life and vitality. As long as this trend continues, we will experience a steady and deliberate march into social and spiritual darkness.

PART
TWO

Heart
Failure

5

The Darkness
of Our Times

But mark this:
There will be terrible times in the last days.
—2 TIMOTHY 3:1 NIV

THE SPIRITUAL VACUUM OF OUR TIMES IS BEING
filled with the subtle darkness of evil. We are no longer a
predominantly Christian society. The symbols and trap-
pings of Christianity remain in some cases, but the heart
and soul of our country's faith have been polluted by the
secular pursuit of life without God. More and more, it is
evident that the majority of people are looking in all the
wrong places to find meaning and purpose to their lives.

Aleksandr Solzhenitsyn has remarked, "The forces of Evil
have begun their decisive offensive."[1] So it seems that we are

digging in for what may well be the final onslaught against biblical Christianity. The final blow may not come from a direct offensive of anti-Christian sentiment, but from sheer neglect of its message. After all, what better way to undermine the gospel than to live as though it did not exist?

We see evidence of that neglect in every form of art, music, literature, and film. Many of the artists and writers are void of spiritual values, conflicts, and concerns. They are so ignorant of biblical truth that they go about their lives as if there was no God. The movies are full of characters like the one portrayed by Michael Douglas in *Wall Street*, who bellows out, "Greed is good! Greed works!" Then there is the proverbial prostitute characterized by Julia Roberts in *Pretty Woman*, who defends her profession with the inane remark, "You gotta make a living."

These are just a few of the many examples of non-Christian or even anti-Christian sentiment that predominate modern culture. There are still many genuine believers who have not capitulated to secularism, materialism, and pragmatism. But all too often, these attitudes can be found even within the Christian community. It is as though the darkness is so great that even we can't always find our way through the maze of modern life.

We have every convenience conceivable to make our lives easier. Jet airplanes speed us across the country and around the world in a matter of hours. Satellite television transmissions bring world events to us within seconds. Air conditioning cools us in the summer; central heating warms us in the winter. Life is no longer a struggle for raw survival. It is often the pursuit of life, liberty, and happiness just as our forefathers planned.

But the freedom to pursue life often allows us to become sidetracked from its true meaning and purpose. Most people are so busy these days that they can't sit still long enough to enjoy the life they have. Most of us over-extend and overcommit ourselves to the point that even our leisure time often increases our stress.

THE NEW DARK AGES

Charles Colson has noted that the church had to stand alone against the barbarian culture of the Dark Ages.[2] Classical Rome had become corrupt from within and fell to the waves of warring bands of illiterate barbarian tribes. Medieval Europe lay in the shambles of spiritual darkness, but the church fought illiteracy, moral degradation, and political corruption. The barbarians could not withstand the stubborn resistance of Christian civilization. In time, Europe emerged from the Dark Ages into an era of spiritual and intellectual creativity and growth.

Colson sees the church at the same crisis point today—confronting the new Dark Ages. The Bible predicts that a time of spiritual apostasy will precede the revealing of the Antichrist ("man of sin").[3] The book of Revelation describes this apostasy as the religion of the "great whore." She is the epitome of false religion and spiritual adultery. By contrast, the New Testament church is pictured as a virgin betrothed to Christ.

Most evangelicals believe this apostasy is made up of people who outwardly profess Christianity but have no inward possession of the Spirit of God. The apostate whore is not made up of any particular denomination, but of all those who do not truly love the Lord. Many view the false religion of the last days as a combination of corrupted Roman Catholicism, liberal Protestantism, New Age mysticism, and materialistic evangelicalism all rolled into one grand deception.[4]

Years ago, professing Christians almost always acknowledged the authority of Scripture. Whether they were willing to live by it or not, people believed the legitimacy of biblical morality. Today, that is often not the case. Even professing evangelical believers will often disregard the commands of God. It is typical today for people to respond with an "I don't care" attitude when confronted with biblical truth. People used to say, "Pastor, I know what I'm doing is wrong, but I just can't help myself." Today, the more common response is, "I know what the Bible says, but I'm going to do what I want."

This shift of attitude betrays the self-oriented mind-set

that is so prevalent in our modern culture. People want what is best for themselves regardless of whom they hurt or what moral principles they violate.

SPIRIT OF ANTICHRIST

There is no doubt in my mind that the stage is set for the final rise of apostasy. The apostle John warned centuries ago that the spirit of Antichrist is already at work through the lust of the flesh, the lust of the eyes, and the pride of life. He added that there are "many antichrists" who "went out from us" because they "were not of us" (1 John 2:16–19; 4:1–4).

Professing Christians who really do not know Christ and do not possess His Spirit are called "little antichrists" because they express the spirit and attitude of Antichrist. But they only *prefigure* the Antichrist, who is described in the Bible as the "man of sin," the "son of perdition," and the "beast out of the sea."

The idea that such a great deceiver could come upon the world scene instantly and dramatically may seem remote to some, but many New Agers have already proposed such a possibility. Barbara Marx Hubbard, executive director of the World Future Society and a Democratic Party nominee for vice president of the United States in 1984, believes that a mass transformation could trigger a "planetary Pentecost" that would empower millions of people at once in a quantum leap toward world wholeness.[5] Hubbard sees this as "the great instant of cooperation" that will be triggered by some great cosmic event.

Many evangelicals believe the rapture of the church will be just such an event! It will have global significance and proportions that will shake the entire world population. Thus, it will have to be explained in some manner. The Bible warns that explanation will be a lie that brings "powerful delusion" to the unbelieving world (2 Thessalonians 2:11 NIV). Whether New Age prophecies are setting the stage for this deception, only time will tell. But the mindset of New Age thinking certainly comes dangerously closer to this than anything we have seen before.

LEFT BEHIND

While the anticipation of Christ's coming to rapture the church is the blessed hope of the believer, it is a sobering matter for those who are left behind. They are described as the deceived unbelievers who have no hope. They will succumb to the great lie and will perish and be damned (2 Thessalonians 2:10–12). This is not a pretty picture, but it is God's warning to a defiant and unbelieving world.

When the Antichrist rises to power, he will oppose God, exalt himself above God, and even claim to be God (2 Thessalonians 2:4). The Bible warns us that the

Antichrist will be empowered by Satan to do miracles of signs and wonders (2 Thessalonians 2:9). He will be assisted by the False Prophet who encourages the worship of the Antichrist as God.

The description of the reign of the Antichrist in biblical prophecy indicates a one-world system in the final days. The Antichrist will deceive the world and control the world's economy. Thus, no one can buy or sell except those who have "the mark or the name of the beast, or the number of his name" (Revelation 13:17). Those who are left behind at the rapture are caught in the global system and cannot escape.

This entire period of time is described as the tribulation. It is a time of trouble for the whole world. The Bible predicts that during this time a third of the trees and all of the grass will be burned up. It predicts air pollution, water pollution, earthquakes, war, and total chaos (see Revelation 6:12–14; 8:7–12). At least one-third of mankind will die during this time (Revelation 9:15).

We can only guess how and when this deception will begin to occur. But even the most skeptical mind must admit that our concepts of truth and reality have changed drastically in the past fifty years. People are no longer concerned about what is true; rather, they want to know what works for them.

The powerful and revealing book *The Agony of Deceit,*

edited by Michael Horton, provides vivid details of the erroneous and even heretical ideas being promoted by some preachers.[6] The tragedy of our times is that even well-intentioned believers are often caught up in doctrinal error and don't even know it. Every human being is vulnerable to error, but when the ultimate deception comes, few will be able to withstand it. This is why a knowledge of the Bible is necessary to offset erroneous ideas. People who are immersed in secularism have no defense against spiritual deception.

WHOSE FAULT IS IT?

The Roman orator Cicero once said, "It is impossible to know the truth and not be held responsible." Yet today we find millions of Americans who realize something has gone wrong in our country, but they have not taken the initiative to find out what it is or what to do about it. Too many Americans blame the politicians for the sad state of affairs we are in today, but it is we, the American people, who have allowed these conditions to exist. Many have protested pornography, homosexuality, abortion, and other moral and social ills, yet they still permeate our society. The real root of our national decay is moral and spiritual. This has resulted in decadence in every area of American life—economics, business, politics, and public life in general.

Over a decade ago, Marvin Stone observed the growing trend of callousness in our society. He observed, "We shrug off almost everything now, moving on to the next fleeting titillation. It's as if we are beyond making distinctions, beyond caring . . . After two centuries we have reached a consensus of indifference."[7]

The real tragedy of our times is that people have almost totally neglected the spiritual values that made our country great, while pursuing the temporal and material values that can never bring lasting satisfaction to the human soul. Man was created in the image of God with a God-consciousness. Ultimately, we can only be satisfied by knowing, loving, and serving God. Every other approach to life degenerates into the mindless pursuit of self-interest and self-gratification.

Drug addiction and alcoholism are still prevalent in our society. People are spending their lives and their money lusting after things that can never satisfy their deepest needs. We live in a twisted world of depressed people who have violated divine laws and are now suffering the consequences of guilt, confusion, and emptiness.

IS THERE ANY HOPE?

Sin is the transgression of God's law. When a person does what is right in his own eyes, he is really saying that it does not matter to him what God thinks about it. The Bible reminds us, "Righteousness exalts a nation, but sin is a reproach to any people" (Proverbs 14:34). People or nations cannot ignore God's laws, live as they please, and expect to be happy and blessed. This does not mean that God gloats in His judgments, because He does not. God's heart is broken over our sins, and His punishments are meant to correct us and bring us to repentance.

God gave Israel a wonderful promise: "If My people who are called by My name will humble themselves, and pray and seek My face, and turn from their wicked ways, then I will hear from heaven and will forgive their sin and heal their land" (2 Chronicles 7:14). As Christians living at the dawn of the twenty-first century, we must again repent and turn to God, believing that He will forgive our sins and heal our land.

Many have forgotten God's gracious intervention. Others have neglected their promises to God. The time has come for another clarion call to revival among God's people. Our political leaders may help or hinder that process, but the future of America is not in their hands. God's people are the only ones who can make a lasting difference, and that not of ourselves, but by the grace of God. As the Lord directs and guides us, we can be the light of the world in a time of spiritual darkness.

TAKING A STAND

It is never popular to stand against trends of the time, but that is exactly what we are often called to do. If Bible-believing Christians are not willing to stand up for biblical morality, who will?

The ongoing abortion debate gives us a chilling example.

Regardless of popular belief, the truth is, human life is precious to God. Jesus Christ died upon the cross for every human being. The Christian heritage in America has emphasized the dignity of human life. We have been known as a nation that honors and protects the right to life, but our national tolerance of abortion is causing us to lose respect for the sanctity of life. More babies have been legally murdered by abortion since 1973 than the total number of Americans killed in all the wars in our nation's history.

Ironically, many of those who defend and promote abortion are the very same people who turn right around and want to protect baby whales, spotted owls, wolves, and eagles' eggs. Only a morally perverted society would value animal life above human life. Certainly we ought to be concerned about the natural environment. I believe we ought to do all we can to prevent the extinction of various species—but not at the expense of human life! Abortionists will never convince me that I should be more concerned about a baby whale than a baby boy or girl.

The searing of the American conscience on the issue of abortion only opens the door to further atrocities like infanticide and euthanasia. Dr. C. Everett Koop, former U.S. surgeon general, and the late Dr. Francis Schaeffer put it this way: "Once the uniqueness of people as created by God is removed . . . there is no reason not to treat people as things to be experimented on . . . If people are not unique, as made in the image of God, the barrier is gone . . . Will a society which has assumed the right to kill infants in the womb— because they are unwanted, imperfect, or merely inconvenient—have difficulty in assuming the right to kill other human beings, especially older adults who are judged unwanted, imperfect, or a social nuisance?"[8]

It is a known fact of history that Adolf Hitler ordered the abortion of babies whose expectant mothers had a history of genetic defects long before he began the genocide of the Jews whom he considered genetically defective. Once a few people have the power to decide which life and whose life may be eliminated, anything can be legitimatized in the name of rights, freedoms, or the good of the state.

The same arguments are used to justify pornography. Under the false guise of First Amendment rights, every imaginable kind of sexual perversion has been exploited by pornographic books, magazines, and films. *Playboy* magazine brought sex into the drugstores in the 1950s. R- and X-rated movies brought it to the movie screens in the 1960s and 1970s. Cable television brought it into the American home in the 1980s. Today the media provides a daily menu of perversion to undermine the American family.

After so many years of this kind of exposure to sexual lust, violence, and permissiveness, it is no wonder we are in such a moral quagmire today. Sex is no longer viewed as a sacred bond between a husband and wife. Instead, it is promoted as a recreational alternative for consenting partners of any type. Women are tragically demeaned. The privacy of sex is destroyed, and true intimacy is lost.

EMPTINESS OF OUR TIMES

Ours has often been characterized as an empty and meaningless generation. This is a direct result of our culture's habit of neglecting the heart. We follow our heart's basic fleshly desires, paying no heed to the command to guard it against evil. As a result, the mindless pursuit of personal pleasure and the abandonment of God's moral laws have left millions of people desolate, desperately seeking real satisfaction in their lives. The prevailing atmosphere of sexual license has eroded the true meaning of life itself. Tragically, the basic human needs for love, acceptance, companionship, intimacy, and personal affirmation are totally lost in the pursuit of lust, sex, and perversion.

Everything that people really need spiritually and psychologically is lost when God is left out. He and He alone can fill the spiritual vacuum of the human soul. He and He alone can give us the love and acceptance we really need.

I am amazed how many people risk their marriages, their families, their jobs, their security, and their own integrity for a moment of pleasure. Their excuse is usually stated as looking for love, happiness, and acceptance. Yet, those are the very things God promises to give us. "Wasn't God enough?" I want to ask them. "Why did you think someone else could fill that void in your life if God could not?"

There is something fundamentally wrong with our culture. We have more conveniences, more technology, and more leisure time than any society has ever had, and yet most people today are not happy! When will we learn that things will not make us happy? Only God can satisfy the human heart's longing for true joy and happiness. Jesus said, "I have come that they may have life, and have it to the full" (John 10:10 NIV).

Our generation must face the fact that life only works when it is lived God's way. As long as we continue seeking the meaning and purpose of life without God, we will never find it. Only when men and women come to the end of themselves and turn to God will they find the true meaning of life.

6

The Ultimate Deception

*Watch out that no one deceives you . . . False prophets will
appear and deceive many people.*
—MATTHEW 24:4, 11 NIV

THE TURNING POINT FOR MANY PEOPLE WHO LOSE
the battle for the heart comes the moment they are
deceived. And it happens quicker than you might imagine.

No one experiences this more subtly than those
involved in cults. Kelly, Dave, and Chris were students at
the University of Illinois. Each came from a different back-
ground, and each got hooked by a cult masquerading as a
campus Bible study. Today all three are free and living lives
for Christ.

"The preaching was powerful and convincing. Like the

man was an angel from God," Kelly said later. "I'm sure that's what tricked me."

David's explanation of what happened was somewhat different. "I joined their Bible study searching for truth," he said. "I was burned out on the secularism in my college classes. I thought this would help me spiritually. I had no idea it was a religious cult."

Chris joined because his friends joined. But he never felt right about the group's beliefs. "It was like you could sense something was wrong, but you couldn't explain it."

Kelly remembers the turning point. "We sang and prayed a lot, and it seemed like one big spiritual family," she said. "Until they tried to keep us away from our families and friends."

"I got real concerned when they started talking about defending themselves against government intrusion." David admits today. "I knew then it was time to get out!"

Spiritual deception is not a new phenomenon. False prophets have been around as long as there have been legitimate prophets of God. Centuries ago, Moses raised the question to the children of Israel: "How can we know when a message has not been spoken by the LORD?" His answer was, "If what a prophet proclaims in the name of the LORD does not take place or come true, that is a message the LORD has not spoken. That prophet has spoken presumptuously.

Do not be afraid of him" (Deuteronomy 18:21–22 NIV). A true prophet must do the following:

1. Speak in the name of the Lord, not some other god.

2. Have a message that is in accord with God's revealed truth in Scripture.

3. Give predictions of future events that come true *exactly* as stated.

One of the most scathing denunciations of false prophets in all of Scripture is delivered by the prophet Jeremiah. In his time, Jeremiah had to deal constantly with false prophets who opposed his ministry, contradicted his message, and even conspired to have him killed. They kept telling the leaders of Jerusalem that the people had nothing to fear from the Babylonian invaders, but Jeremiah knew differently. Jerusalem was on the verge of destruction, and the people were about to be taken into captivity for seventy years.

"My heart is broken within me," Jeremiah confesses in his agony over these false prophets who ". . . follow an evil course and use their power unjustly" (Jeremiah 23:9–10 NIV). "Both prophet and priest are godless," the Lord responds (23:11 NIV). Then He tells Jeremiah His opinion of these false prophets:

Do not listen to what the prophets are prophesying to you; they fill you with false hopes. They speak visions from their own minds, not from the mouth of the LORD. (verse 16 NIV)

I did not send these prophets, yet they have run with their message; I did not speak to them, yet they have prophesied. (verse 21 NIV)

I have heard what the prophets say who prophesy lies in my name. They say, "I had a dream! I had a dream!" How long will this continue in the hearts of these lying prophets, who prophesy the delusions of their own minds? (verse 25 NIV)

Yes . . . I am against the prophets who wag their own tongues . . . Indeed, I am against those who prophesy false dreams . . . Because every man's own word becomes his oracle and so you distort the words of the living God, the Lord almighty, our God. (verses 31–32, 36 NIV)

Jeremiah could not make his complaint any clearer or his case any stronger. God is against those false prophets whose spiritual delusion causes them to invent their own message apart from God's truth. The Bible presents these people in seven categories:

1. Self-deceived. Some false teachers may be sincere, but they are still wrong. They have deceived themselves into believing their messages are true. As Jeremiah points out, their messages come psychologically from within their own minds and are not from God.

2. Liars. Some false prophets are deliberate liars who have no intention of telling the truth. The apostle John says, "Who is a liar? but he who denies that Jesus is the Christ? He is antichrist who denies the Father and the Son" (1 John 2:22).

3. Heretics. These are they who preach heresy (false doctrine) and divide the church. Of them John said, "They went out from us, but they did not really belong to us" (1 John 2:19 NIV). The apostle Peter said, "There will be false teachers among you, who will secretly bring in destructive heresies . . . These . . . speak evil of the things they do not understand" (2 Peter 2:1, 12).

4. Scoffers. There are some who do not necessarily promote false teaching so much as they outright reject the truth of God. Of them the Bible warns, "Scoffers will come in the last days, walking according to their own lusts" (2 Peter 3:3). The apostle Paul calls them "lovers of themselves . . . boasters, proud" (2 Timothy 3:2). Jude calls them "grumblers and faultfinders" (Jude 16 NIV).

5. Blasphemers. Those who speak evil of God, Christ, the Holy Spirit, the people of God, the kingdom of God, and the attributes of God are called *blasphemers.* Jude calls them godless men who "speak abusively against whatever they do not understand . . . They are clouds without rain . . . trees, without fruit . . . They are wild waves of the sea . . . wandering stars" (Jude 10, 12–13 NIV). The apostle Paul says that he himself was a blasphemer before his conversion to Christ (1 Timothy 1:13).

6. Seducers. Jesus warned that some false prophets will appear with miraculous signs and wonders to seduce or deceive the very elect, if that were possible (Mark 13:22). Our Lord's implication is that spiritual seduction is a very real threat even to believers. This would account for the fact that a few genuine but deceived believers may be found among the cults.

7. Reprobates. This term means "disapproved," "depraved," or "rejected." Paul refers to those who have rejected the truth of God and turned to spiritual darkness. Consequently, God has given them over to a "reprobate mind" (Romans 1:28 KJV). They have so deliberately rejected God that they have become "filled with every kind of wickedness" (verse 29 NIV). As a result, they are "haters of God" (verse 30), whose behavior is "senseless, faithless, heartless, ruthless" (verse 31 NIV). These people are so far gone spiritually that they know it and don't care. In Jesus' own prophetic message, the Olivet Discourse,

He warned, "Watch out that no one deceives you . . . Many will turn away from the faith . . . And many false prophets will appear and deceive many people . . . For false Christs and false prophets will appear and perform great signs and miracles" (Matthew 24:4, 10–11, 24 NIV). Our Lord warned His disciples of the possibility of spiritual seduction by false prophets.

THE MASTER OF DECEIT

The Bible describes Satan as the father of lies (John 8:44) and pictures him as the ultimate deceiver. His name means "accuser," and he is depicted as the accuser of God and His people (Revelation 12:10). He is opposed to God and seeks to alienate people from the truth. He misled the fallen angels (Revelation 12:3–4). He tempts men and women to sin against God's laws (Genesis 3:1–13; 1 Timothy 6:9). He denies and rejects the truth of God and deceives those who perish without God (2 Thessalonians 2:10). Ultimately, he inspires the false prophets and the very spirit of Antichrist (1 John 2:18–23).

The Bible clearly warns us that in the last days people will "depart from the faith, giving heed to deceiving [seducing, KJV] spirits and doctrines of demons" (1 Timothy 4:1). These false teachings will come through hypocritical liars, whose minds have been captured by the following participants of evil:

Satan
Father of Lies

Demons
Doctrines of Devils

False Teachers
Messengers of Deceit

These will all speak Satan's lies (1 Timothy 4:2). Thus, the process of spiritual deception is clearly outlined in Scripture:

The term *angel* (Greek, *angelos*) means "messenger." God's angels are His divine messengers (Hebrews 1:14; Revelation 1:1), and His true prophets and preachers are called the angels of the churches (Revelation 2:1, 8, 12, 18; 3:1, 7, 14). By contrast, Satan is pictured as a fallen angel, the leader of other fallen angels, who deceives the world (Revelation 12:9). He is revealed as the ultimate power behind the Antichrist and the False Prophet who deceives mankind with false religion (Revelation 13:14–15). Thus, the messengers (angels) of deceit are Satan-inspired false prophets and teachers whose messages are the very spirit of Antichrist.

A century ago, A. T. Pierson, the Bible teacher who often spoke for Charles Spurgeon at the Metropolitan

Tabernacle in London, wrote, "Evil spirits acquire their greatest power from their subtilty. They are *masters of the art of deception,* and aim to counterfeit that which is good rather than suggest what is obviously and wholly evil."[1]

SPIRITUAL DECEPTION

The lure of false doctrine is that it presents itself as the truth. It appears as a corrective measure to established doctrine. It is propagated by those who are certain they have discovered some new revelation of truth or a better interpretation of old, established truth. Either way, they are convinced they are right and everyone else is wrong.

This is Satan's oldest trick. He appeals to our self-conceit and leads us into self-deceit. When he first approached Eve, Satan questioned the integrity of God's command and appealed to her selfish desire to be like God—the same desire that led to his own fall. And there is something selfish enough in all of us to want to believe that we can know what no one else knows. C. S. Lewis said:

> What Satan put into the heads of our remote ancestors was the idea that they could "be like gods" . . . Out of that hopeless attempt has come nearly all that we can call human history . . . the long terrible story of man trying to find something other than God which will make him happy.[2]

One does not have to look hard to find expressions of self-centeredness in most cult leaders: Father Devine said he was God. David Koresh claimed to be Jesus Christ. Sun Myung Moon says he is "Lord of the Universe." Herbert W. Armstrong claimed his church was the only one on earth proclaiming "the very same gospel that Jesus taught and proclaimed."

Once the false teacher falls into the *illusion* that he or she alone is God's messenger and has a corner on His truth, spiritual deception is inevitable. Once spiritual deception sets in, it leads to spiritual darkness. It is not long before the deceived cult leader begins to espouse heretical doctrine. Since he or she acknowledges no one else as God's spokesperson, traditional and orthodox concepts may be challenged or even disregarded.[3]

Pride and arrogance are the sins that lead a person to become spiritually deceived. These sins take us to the second stage of spiritual deception. Satan tempts us with our own self-centeredness and lures us into spiritual darkness with the bait of our own pride. We really want to believe we are right and everybody else is wrong. The Bible calls this the "pride of life" (1 John 2:16).

Having been hooked by our arrogance, we are reeled in by our ignorance. Most people who fall into the trap of false doctrine are ignorant of the implications of other views. Many sincere preachers get off the theological track because they don't know enough theology to realize their errors.[4]

The real problem comes when false teachers love their erroneous teaching to the point that they will not repent of it even when their error is exposed. This is what leads to spiritual darkness. The willful rejection of the truth results in the mind being blinded by Satan. The Bible says, "They are darkened in their understanding and separated from the life of God because of the ignorance that is in them due to the hardening of their hearts" (Ephesians 4:18 NIV).

Scripture further explains that Satan himself is the source of spiritual darkness: "The god of this age has blinded the minds of unbelievers, so that they cannot see the light of the gospel of the glory of Christ, who is the image of God" (2 Corinthians 4:4).

Once theological error falls into "ecclesiastical cement" it is virtually impossible to eliminate it. When false doctrine is accepted by an organized religious body, it will be perpetrated by a false defense (apologetic) based upon a false premise. If I honestly believe my dog is a reincarnation of my Uncle Joe, I will look for every possible proof of Uncle Joe's personality in my dog's behavior. When a whole group of followers accept false doctrine as truth, they will organize it, categorize it, and systematize it. But that doesn't make it true!

For example, if I start driving north from Atlanta on I-75, but I really believe I'm heading south, I am not going to end up in Florida no matter what I think. The spiritually deceived person can believe Jesus returned in 1914, or moved into the heavenly temple in 1844, or that He is coming back this year. But just believing it doesn't make it so. My faith has to be anchored in the truth if it is going to do me any good.

APOSTATE RELIGION

Jesus spoke often of false prophets and spiritual deception. He told His disciples that spiritual truth could be recognized by its fruits. Then He added, "Not everyone who says to me, 'Lord, Lord,' will enter the kingdom of heaven . . . Many will say to me on that day, 'Lord, Lord, did we not prophesy in your name, and in your name drive out demons and perform many miracles?' Then I will tell them plainly, 'I never knew you. Away from me, you evildoers!'" (Matthew 7:21–23 NIV).

False religion can arise from any source. Hindu-based cults have produced an endless stream of gurus who claim to be *avatars* (incarnations of deity). Sai Baba says he is the living incarnation of both Jesus and Krishna! Extremist Muslims exist, such as Sheik Oman Abdel-Rahman, the deported cleric whose followers car-bombed the World Trade Center in New York City. Theirs is a gospel of hatred, violence, and murder in the name of God. Jewish

Lubavitchers still believe the late Menachem Schneerson is the Messiah, and are awaiting his return.

One might expect false prophets and extremist cults to arise from non-Christian religions that reject Jesus Christ. But when false cults arise from within Christianity, it is especially disturbing. The New Testament is filled with warnings about heretics, false prophets, and false prophecies. Even in apostolic times, John wrote, "Dear children, this is the last hour; and as you have heard that the antichrist is coming, even now many antichrists have come . . . They went out from us, but they did not really belong to us" (1 John 2:18–19 NIV).

One only has to consider the fiery finale of the Branch Davidian cult led by David Koresh to see the powerful influence of false doctrine. Koresh convinced his followers that he alone could properly interpret the seven seals of the book of Revelation. By "opening" the seals, he further convinced them that he was the Lamb of God—Jesus Christ in the flesh. Therefore, his conflicts with law enforcement agencies were setting the stage for the final battle—Armageddon. He was so self-centered, *Newsweek* noted, "he was consumed by Armageddon and his role in it."[5]

Arguments may persist for some time as to whether the inferno was the result of a mass suicide, an accident, or an act of desperate self-destruction. But the whole terrible mess was the end result of a false prophet whose deceived followers perished for a lie.

It is never the will of God to defend the faith with guns and bullets. Peter attempted to defend Jesus from arrest by the Roman soldiers in the Garden of Gethsemane. Our Lord told Peter to put away his sword because "all who take the sword will perish by the sword" (Matthew 26:52). Later, when Pilate questioned Jesus about being a king, the Lord replied, "My kingdom is not of this world. If it were, my servants would fight to prevent my arrest" (John 18:36 NIV).

A false prophet is one who contradicts the true message of Christ, as well as one whose predictions fail to come true. David Koresh was guilty on both counts. A typically self-deceived extremist cult leader, Koresh perished with nearly ninety of his followers in the flames at Ranch Apocalypse. But in Matthew 23:25–33, Jesus Christ warned there is a worse fate for false teachers: They will not escape the fires of hell!

THE CULTIC MIND

The general public was shocked when the author of an academic bestseller argued that modern students have now abandoned rational inquiry for relativism, replacing reason with emotion.[6] Today's students, he observed, don't care what is right or wrong so long as it works. They are more interested in pursuing the good life than in making right decisions. Students who are a product of modern education are not committed to noble ideas and therefore are incapable of developing noble goals.[7] Since relativity prevails, students are robbed of their spiritual values and are left with an overload of information that cannot change their lives.[8]

It is into this moral and intellectual vacuum that the cults make their greatest appeal to today's generation. They appear to offer answers to life's questions. They provide a structure for moral choices, and they demand allegiance to a great cause. But, unlike genuine Christianity, the cults recruit through deception and hold their converts by manipulation. Just try to get the guy selling flowers at the airport and other public places to tell you to which group he belongs. He won't do it. Ask those inviting you to a Bible study or campus group to tell you up-front with whom or what they are associated. If they hesitate or are vague, they probably have something to hide.

In his powerful and insightful book *Unholy Devotion: Why Cults Lure Christians,* Harold Bussell makes these crucial observations about false cults:[9]

1. They gain control of their followers by demanding that they surrender control of their lives. This surrender is to be done to the cult itself in order to meet one's needs and accomplish one's goals. This is generally done under the guise of surrendering all to some higher being. In occult circles, the ultimate surrender is to Satan himself!

2. Their manipulation bases its appeal more on emotion than logic. Bussell notes that people today are more persuaded by the dynamics of a speaker's personality or delivery than they are by the content of his message. This means that even well-educated people can be easily manipulated by powerful appearances, dynamic messages, and emotional experiences.

3. They offer strict guidelines for acceptable behavior. To a morally bankrupt and confused society, most cults offer very rigid guidelines for moral behavior. The cults demand allegiance to a code of conduct that locks the followers into the group. Since no one else makes such demands, it is assumed they must be right. Following that logic, the cult can demand almost anything from its followers, who will give up everything to satisfy the convictions of the cult.

4. They often excuse the behavior of their leaders. The rigid demands of cults are so difficult to maintain that even their leaders often fall short. But instead of honest admissions, true confessions, or genuine repentances, the cults often try to excuse or cover up their leaders' failures. Mormons don't want to talk about Joseph Smith's polygamy. Jehovah's Witnesses never mention Charles Russell's divorce. And nobody at the Jim Jones's People's

Temple talked about those Kool-Aid communion services until it was too late!

The ultimate hook of the cultic mentality is that of perpetual obligation. The cultist is never free from the cult. The assurance of salvation is never fully realized. The devotee must pray better, witness more, meditate longer, try harder, and work endlessly. Promoters of false religion leave their followers in total dependence upon themselves. They are devoid of any theological structure or biblical truth that offers a sure and lasting salvation.

David Breese makes the insightful observation in his book *The Marks of a Cult* that cultists are kept in hopeless bondage to the cult.[10] He observes that Jehovah's Witnesses are never quite sure if they are one of the 144,000. New Agers who believe in reincarnation are never sure whether they are coming back or going on ahead to something better. Krishna devotees live in constant fear of losing their Krishna-consciousness and failing to merge with deity.

Breese comments, "A thoughtful person who examines the preaching and writing of the cults carefully is almost certain to sense a frustrating indefiniteness. He is being strung along, beguiled up a primrose path to nowhere."[11] In contrast to the uncertainty of the cultic appeal, consider the striking words of the apostle Paul, who said, "I know whom I have believed, and am persuaded that he is able to keep that which I have committed unto him against that day" (2 Timothy 1:12 KJV).

THE BIG LIE

Most cults bind their converts by the lie that they alone have the truth and, therefore, they are the only true people of God. Tragically, this idea often begins with sincere self-deception. Many cult leaders actually believe they have discovered the truth that others fail to see. Therefore they quickly conclude they are the only ones who know the truth.

Once the cultist buys the lie that "we" alone are right and all others are wrong, spiritual pride and arrogance set in quickly. Since the cult alone has the truth, it can judge all other beliefs as erroneous. All they have to do is evaluate the claims of others in comparison with their own beliefs. Any discrepancy is viewed as a departure from the truth (as understood by the cult). Detractors are quickly denounced as heretics, liars, and deceivers.

The acceptance of the lies that "we alone are God's people" and "we alone know the truth" leads to the abandonment of one's self to the exaggerated claims of the cult leader ("I am God" or "I alone can lead you to God"). This, in turn, immerses the devotee into the mind-set of the cult, which becomes his or her new world.

Each cult has a vocabulary unique to itself. The longer the

convert is isolated by the group, the more he or she will begin to think and talk in the terminology of the cult. In time, new concepts fill one's conversations: *holy discourses, heavenly handshake, dreamless sleep, the force, spirit guides, heavenly deception, according to principle, spoiling the system, harmonic convergence, karma, mantras, millennial dawn, Nephites, telestial Kingdom, devas, mahatmas, flirty fishing,* and *animal magnetism* become designations, code words, and shibboleths used by cult insiders.

Unfortunately, most cult evangelists don't begin by emphasizing the unique and bizarre elements of their cult's doctrine. Rather, they tend to start with commonly used religious terminology. Many talk of finding inner peace, spiritual help, and personal salvation. Some are big on morality and family. Others are concerned about Bible prophecy, and appeal to one's need to understand the future. Some emphasize the power of the mind, which tends to appeal to intellectuals. Others want to help you find yourself by finding their concept of God.

THE FINAL TRAP

All this may sound rather harmless at first, but it becomes the hook that lures the potential convert into the cultic world. The extremist cults then take total control of the convert's life. Some insist that all one's possessions be donated to the cause. Some determine whom you can marry, where you can live, and what time you should get up in the morning. The more general cults allow members to possess their own property, live in their own homes, and make their own daily decisions. But they also tend to exert strong control through guilt manipulation, personal intimidation, and even social rejection and shunning.

The cult member ends up being intimidated by such threats only because he or she has already believed it! The acceptance of the basic cult lie ("we alone are God's true people") leads to uncritical allegiance to leadership ("I am God's only true spokesperson"), and the rest is automatic! Hence, some believe demons sit on their eyelids to make them sleep during lectures because that is what their leaders teach.[12] Many New Agers believe they are reincarnations of famous people because their leaders believe it about themselves.[13] Some cults won't salute the flag or serve in the military because their leaders believe that Christ has already returned and set up His kingdom, which supersedes all human governments. Believing the Church Age to have ended in 1914, they meet in kingdom halls and denounce all churches as apostate.

Once you accept the premise of false teaching, all the rest falls consistently in line. Believing the basic lie, one closes his mind to the truth and throws away the key of logic. From that point on, anything and everything can and will make sense to the cultic mentality—even worshiping the Antichrist!

7

The Erosion of Truth

*Because of the increase of wickedness the
love of most will grow cold.*
—*MATTHEW 24:12 NIV*

IT WAS LATE AT NIGHT IN THE FRATERNITY HOUSE
and Chris and Tim were laying on the couches talking.

"I don't know what to believe anymore," Chris admitted.
"So many opinions, ideas, and options. I'm tired of trying to
figure it out! I want to live my own life and be left alone."

"You used to talk about God this and God that." Tim
flopped onto his back and stared at the ceiling. "All that
stuff about how I should find God and then I'd have all the
answers. Remember?"

Chris released a drawn-out sigh through clenched teeth.

"I remember." He propped his head up with a nearby pillow. "But these days God seems so far away—especially on campus. I get tired of having my faith ridiculed and bombarded in class every day. It'd be easier not to believe anything. Then nobody would care."

God never promised that things would get easier as we neared the end of the age. In fact, many of us believe that things will get worse before they get better. The assault on the heart during the last century has left our society cold, empty, and hollow. We have the best that technology can provide, but we are not happy with ourselves. We are desperately trying to make ourselves happy. But we are running away as fast as we can from the only One who can really give us true happiness.

The twentieth century brought the most incredible changes imaginable to the human race. Automobiles, airplanes, radios, television, and computers have thrust us into an environment our forefathers never could have envisioned. Whether we like it or not, each one of us is affected by modern technology daily, and that technology is shaping our lives. It is no wonder that historian Paul Johnson called these days "modern times."[1]

Yet, with the advancement of modernity has come a restless uneasiness about the traditional values that are slipping away from our society. At times consciously and at other times unconsciously, we seem to be discarding the very ideas that built this great society. It would even seem that we have exchanged our souls for a technological mess of pottage.

As the twentieth century sped along, secularism began to replace the Judeo-Christian values of our society. God was gradually but systematically removed from any place of prominence in our intellectual lives. Scientism emerged, turning pure science into a religion, which taught that natural laws, not spiritual principles, guided the universe.[2]

The entrenchment of the theory of evolution made God unnecessary in our culture. Many people actually felt betrayed because their belief in God had enabled them to believe in their own worth and dignity. Life had meaning and purpose as people lived to bring glory to God. But now those ideas have been swept away by the intellectual broom of secularism. Man now sees himself as little more than a glorified animal whose highest instincts are to satisfy his own selfish desires.

THE REIGN OF RELATIVISM

The philosophical concept that dominates the thinking of people today is *relativism*.[3] It is the opposite of absolutism and teaches that all truth is relative to its context. There are *no absolutes* according to this belief. Absolute truth is an impossibility in a world of relative contingencies. Something is "true" only because a majority of people accept it as truth; all issues are subject to human interpretation at any given point in time. In other words, what is considered to be true in one culture may not be true in another.

Relativism dethrones divine law. It not only rejects the teachings of Scripture as binding upon human behavior, but it even rejects the very concept of scripture. According to relativism, a writing is considered scripture only because a society deems it so. The writing is not viewed as inherently divine in nature. Relativists view the Bible on the same level as the Koran, the Tripitakas of Buddha, or the Hindu Vedas. In some cases, modern critics have even suggested that other writings are superior to the Bible.

The influence of relativism has affected nearly every area of modern thinking. Once one accepts the basic premise of relativism, he no longer views truth as an absolute proposition.[4] The great danger of this concept is that it leads to a naive acceptance of the consequences of secularism. Under this system of thought, even the concepts of good and evil are viewed as culturally conditioned, and therefore relative to the perspective of that culture. Thus, even murder is not considered inherently wrong. It is only wrong because society deems it wrong.

HAVE WE LOST OUR MINDS?

One of the most powerful books to appear in recent times is *The Closing of the American Mind*.[5] Written by Allan

Bloom, a professor of social thought at the University of Chicago, this blockbuster bestseller explores the intellectual vacuum of our time. Bloom argues that today's students are unlike any generation that has preceded them. They are headed, in his opinion, to intellectual oblivion because of the relativism that has permeated our culture.

Bloom calls his volume "a meditation on the state of our souls."[6] Though the book is not written from a Christian standpoint, it raises many issues Christians have been concerned about for years. Bloom argues that students have been so conditioned by our educational system to believe that all truth is relative that they are devoid of absolutes on which to build their lives. As a result, he explains, our culture has drifted with the winds of self-gratification.[7]

Bloom is especially concerned about the self-centeredness of today's students. "Students these days are, in general, nice," he says. But, he adds, "They are not particularly moral or noble." The author observes that they are the product of good times when "neither tyranny nor want has hardened them or made demands on them." As a result, he warns that young people today have abandoned themselves to the pursuit of the "good life."[8]

Unfortunately, the current quest of most students is for money, sex, power, and pleasure. It should not surprise us that these are problems for Christians as well because they are the dead-end options of a society stuck on itself.

Bloom writes, "Country, religion, family, ideas of civilization, all the sentimental and historical forces that stood between cosmic infinity and the individual, providing some notion of a place within the whole, have been rationalized away and have lost their compelling force."[9] He also adds that we are now experiencing what de Tocqueville, the French admirer of American democracy, warned would ultimately lead to the "disappearance of citizens and statesmen." In other words, everybody is caught up in "making it" for himself, and really isn't interested in the common good of others.

The rise of *individualism,* coupled with the decline of the traditional family, has left us with a generation that has a tough time making commitments. This tendency shows up in almost every area of life, from choosing a career, to holding a job, to getting married. Reluctance to commit oneself to a belief or ideal is the inevitable result of relativism in our culture. We have a situation akin to the days of the biblical judges, when "every man did that which was right in his own eyes."

GOING FIRST CLASS ON THE *TITANIC*

Another educator, Arthur Levine, has described the current student mentality as that of going "first class on the *Titanic*."[10] What he means is that students not only have become self-centered, but they have also given up any real hope of solving the world's problems. They view society as a sinking ship that will never reach its ultimate destination; they view themselves as stuck on a hopeless voyage. Since they can't get off, they simply clamor for the first-class seats on the top deck so they can enjoy the ride until disaster strikes. In other words, if they are going to be stuck on the *Titanic,* they intend to make the best of it.

Whether we like it or not, most of us are products of our times. As Christians we must literally fight against the undercurrent of secularism and relativism that is sweeping away our Judeo-Christian foundation. Today's Christian students must be willing to swim upstream against the intellectual tide if they hope to make any real difference in our society. Claiming to be a Christian really isn't enough anymore; we must be willing to show it.

The choices we make regarding the investment of our lives will reflect whether we are committed to ourselves or others. In a time when most people are choosing to live for them-selves, we must be willing to demonstrate the reality of Christ by living for Him and investing ourselves in others. This is the real key to finding meaning and purpose in one's life.

THE APPEASEMENT OF EVIL

The greatest danger of relativism is that it leads to the eventual appeasement of evil. If all truth is relative, then no belief is worth dying for. If I have part of the truth and you have part of the truth, then neither of us has the whole truth. Once we accept this concept, we have no basis upon which to judge actions as morally right or wrong. Thus, it should not surprise us that secular society is willing to tolerate abortion, euthanasia, and even infanticide. The unborn, the elderly, the retarded, and the handicapped all become expendable by such logic.[11]

Former Surgeon General C. Everett Koop calls this indifference to the sanctity of life the "slide to Auschwitz."[12] Once philosophers, theologians, and medical personnel adopt such a view, a growing loss of human dignity will automatically occur. This is the same intellectual journey that led to the acceptance of Hitler's Nazi atrocities. A change in the moral climate toward human life is all that is necessary for the systematic elimination of undesirable life forms to become the norm.

Australian ethicist Peter Singer recently said, "We can no longer base our ethics on the idea that human beings are a special form of creation, made in the image of God, singled out from all other animals, and alone possessing an immortal soul."[13] Commenting on Singer's statement, Cal Thomas observes that removing the protective layer of man's uniqueness leaves him as vulnerable as a dog or a pig in the discussion about who or what ought to live—an assertion that Singer himself makes![14]

In commenting on the seriousness of abortion, Stuart

Briscoe says, "Destruction of that made in the image of God challenges the divine intention. If God makes man for eternity and gives him the ability to function in relationship to Him, anyone who kills that man destroys what God had in mind. The destroyer shakes his fist in the face of God."[15]

A HUMANISTIC VIEW OF GOVERNMENT

Humanism is that form of secularism that views man, not God, as the central reality of life. Gloria Steinem, founding editor of *Ms.* magazine and recipient of the American Humanist Association Pioneer Award, said, "By the twenty-first century we will, I hope, raise our children to believe in human potential, not God."[16] Humanists, in general, believe that people must solve their own problems apart from any divine guidance. Secular humanism and relativism are the philosophic bases of modern liberalism.

Secular humanism is "a God-less, man-centered philosophy of life that rejects moral absolutes and traditional values."[17] Secular humanists have relentlessly sought to secularize our nation by influencing legislative and judicial governmental control in every area of our society, including the church and the family.

R. C. Sproul defines humanism as an *anthropocentric* (man-centered) view of life as opposed to a *theocentric* (God-centered) view of life.[18] He traces its origins to the pre-Socratic Greek philosopher Protagoras, whose motto was *homo mensura,* meaning "man (is) the measure." As a result of its own presuppositions, humanism rejects the concept of divinely revealed moral absolutes and argues for man's right to determine his own morality.

Modern humanism, as reflected in the *Humanist Manifestos* (1933, 1973) and the *Humanist Declaration* (1980), is decidedly anti-Christian in its bias. One leading proponent of humanist education, John Dewey, said, "Religion tends to hinder the evolutionary progress of man."[19] In reality, Francis Schaeffer contended, humanism borrowed the moral concerns of Christianity and tore them loose from their theological foundation. Unless it is stopped, he warned, humanism "intends to beat to death the [Christian] base which made our culture possible."[20]

THE FILTRATION OF IDEAS

The present conflict between religion and politics is not merely a political issue. Rather, it is the last wave of the conflict that has been raging between Christianity and anti-Christianity throughout this century. The first waves of this conflict were philosophical and then theological. As the philosophies of relativism and secularism began to dominate thinking in the late nineteenth century, they soon influenced theology as well. This gave rise to theological liberalism and the eventual ecclesiastical controversies between fundamentalism and modernism.[21]

As the concepts of relativism and secularism gained control of institutionalized religion, they provoked theological debate, which, in turn, led to ecclesiastical power struggles to control the ideology of the mainline denominations. Thus the argumentation shifted to the issue of ecclesiastical control. When conservatives were unable to prevent liberalism from infiltrating and eventually controlling the theological institutions, they withdrew, forming new denominations and new institutions. This left liberalism entrenched in the mainline institutions. As time passed, succeeding generations of theological students became increasingly secularized so that today one cannot distinguish a liberal theological agenda from a secular one.

The influence of nearly a century of liberal preaching has now filtered down to the level of the common person in society. Popular literature, television, and movies all tend to reflect this mentality. As the liberal mind-set gained a grip on society, it also influenced the political process through legislative and judicial change. Political decisions began to reflect the values of secularism.

This process of the *filtration of ideas* was first brought to the attention of evangelicals by the late Francis Schaeffer.[22] He viewed philosophy as the wellspring from which popular culture derived. As philosophical concepts filter down through the culture, they first affect the elite and eventually become popularized by society in general. The process works something like this:

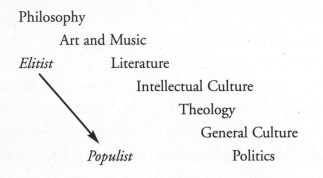

Philosophy

    Art and Music

Elitist   Literature

        Intellectual Culture

          Theology

           General Culture

    Populist   Politics

Filtration of Ideas: From Intellectual Elites to
Popular Culture to Politics

Schaeffer argued that the philosophical concepts of Kant and Hegel gave rise to a whole new way of thinking that resulted in relativism. He suggested that this concept spread geographically from Germany to Holland and Switzerland before it caught on in England and America. It was popularized by French skepticism and German rationalism. As an American living in Switzerland, Schaeffer realized that American culture was moving in the same direction as European culture, though at a slower pace. God was simply being eliminated as a serious intellectual option. Schaeffer also observed that relativism affected the intellectual classes first and was passed on to the workers by the mass media, bypassing the middle class. He observed, "The middle class was not touched by it and often is still not touched by it."[23]

The strength of the evangelical church in America is our greatest deterrent to relativism and secularism. Were it not for the thousands of evangelical churches and schools representing millions of members, secularism would have swept America long ago. This is why there is still a great void between evangelical and liberal churches today. Not only does our theology differ, but our entire response to the modern culture rests upon totally different philosophical foundations.

What was unique about the twentieth century, however, was the ability of the mass media to translate secular values to every level of society through television, films, books, and magazines. Our inability to think critically and objectively while being entertained, especially by television, movies, or videos, leaves even the Christian community vulnerable to the influence of secularism. We can watch a program that challenges or contradicts the very values we hold dear and never even realize it!

POLITICS: CHRISTIANITY'S LAST STAND

The grip of secularism on our society is so tight that its influence is being felt in nearly every area of American life.

The secularization of education, morality, and public policy eventually results in the politicization of those beliefs through the legislative and judicial process. The end result will be the legalization of secularism and the disenfranchisement of Judeo-Christianity.

Politics, in the broadest sense of human governance, is the last line of defense for religion in our society. The filtration of secularism is now so nearly complete that it dares to enshrine itself through the political processes. For example, when evolutionists argued for academic freedom to present the theory of evolution in the public schools at the time of the Scopes Trial in 1925, it was assumed by both sides in the debate that creationism would also be allowed to be taught. In fact, that assumption was so widely held that no one seriously questioned it. All the evolutionists wanted at that time was the opportunity to gain a fair hearing for their position. But in the decades that passed, secularism gained such control of public education that the teaching of creation is now forbidden by law. Creationists do not even have the same fundamental academic freedom for which evolutionists once begged.[24]

One of the peculiarities of a democracy is that it is always in a state of flux. Any particular group can potentially propose new legislation at any time. Therefore, democracies are rarely static; there is nearly always a state of fluidity in the exchange of ideas. Unfortunately, most Christians tend to forget this. We think that things will continue as they have always been. As a result, we live in a naive moment of false security in which we have forgotten the whole history of the world.

A PUBLICLY IRRELEVANT FAITH

While acknowledging his personal concerns about the illusion of political power brokering, Charles Colson admits that we have come to a time when many people are advocating a privately engaging but publicly irrelevant faith.[25] He argues that two extreme positions dominate Christian thinking on the issue of religion and politics. On the one hand, he sees a politicized faith that tends to seek political solutions to spiritual problems while neglecting the church's real spiritual mission. On the other hand, Colson observes a privatized faith that "divorces religious and spiritual beliefs from public actions."[26]

Colson observes that the political left, including mainline religion, has a "morbid fear of religion encroaching on the secular realm."[27] Evangelicals have an equally morbid fear of secularism encroaching on religious freedoms. This is exactly where the controversy between religion and secularism lies today. While mainline religion has an innate fear of imposing religious values in a pluralistic society, evangelicals have an innate fear of allowing secularists to impose antireligious values on that society.

Colson criticized former New York Governor Mario Cuomo for a publicly irrelevant position on abortion. Colson noted that the ex-governor was a practicing Catholic who held to his church's belief that abortion is wrong. As a public official, Cuomo acknowledged in a speech at the University of Notre Dame that he not only could not impose his views on others, but that he was under no obligation to advocate such views either. Such a position, Colson says, is "impotent to reverse the tides of secularism."[28]

Where do the extremes of privatization or politicization leave us? Unfortunately, they tend to leave us in confusion. On the one extreme are Christians who believe we must take over the government in order to enforce religious values. On the other extreme are Christians who pietistically want to avoid all public or political issues. We believe that the church can have a proper balance between these two extremes. We must become a voice of conscience to our society or forever forfeit any spiritual influence in matters of public policy. The fact that religious, spiritual, and moral issues have become a subject of political debate simply indicates how far secularism has already advanced in our society.

The real losers in this contest to capture the heart of American culture are the children. Between kindergarten and grade twelve, the average child is subjected to twelve thousand hours of humanistic indoctrination. As many as half our evangelical young people drop out of church by the time they reach college because they think religion is irrelevant to their lives. One of the greatest challenges facing the church today is to educate the whole child in a combined effort of churches, parents, and Christian schools. Sunday school alone is not enough to offset the influence of a secular education in our public schools.

DRAWING A LINE OF DEFENSE

Much of the evangelical involvement in political issues has been little more than drawing a line of defense against the encroachment of secularism. For the most part, evangelicals have not advocated taking rights away from secularists or humanists. Conservatives have merely insisted that secularists not deny their rights to live by the moral values and principles they believe to be valid. For example, evangelicals are not calling for the elimination of existing rights for anyone. They simply oppose extending those rights to include the imposition of a nonbiblical morality upon the church or church-related institutions.

If we do not draw a line of defense at this point of the debate, we will end up sacrificing everything we believe in the area of public policy. This does not mean that the church cannot survive in a hostile society. In some cases, as in ancient pagan Rome and modern atheistic communism, true Christianity has actually flourished. In other cases, such as under the sword of Islam, it has been eradicated.

Conservative Christians are merely calling the church to awaken to its responsibilities in this opening part of the twenty-first century. There is no excuse for us to lose our religious freedoms in a democratic society. If this does happen, we will have no one to blame but ourselves. The irrelevance of a privatized pietism is as dangerous to the health of Christianity as is the apathy of a self-indulgent church.

Whether we like it or not, we have come to religion's last stand in American culture. The political debate is the final attempt of secularism to prevail over religion in our society. The implications of this debate have eternal consequences. For secularism, all human values must be understood in the present, whereas the biblical world-view is eternal. R. C. Sproul rightly observes, "This is precisely where Christianity and secularism collide. This is the point of conflict."[29] Sproul observes that "right now" counts forever in Christianity. What we do has eternal significance because our existence is related to God Himself.

THE DUST OF DEATH

At the peak of secularization in the 1960s and 1970s, theologians began to talk abut synthesizing Christianity with secularism in the concept of the *death of God*. They viewed

God as having surrendered His transcendence and capitulating to the secular through the incarnation of Christ. When Jesus took on humanity, the transcendent God died, they argued, leaving mankind with the pursuit of its own solutions to its problems.[30]

Sproul again observes, "The death of God, in terms of the loss of transcendence and the loss of the eternal, also means the death of man. It means that history has no transcendent goal. There is no eternal purpose."[31] Once the secular mind-set gains control of the way a society thinks, it will not be long until those thoughts are translated into political structures.

Society is losing its belief in the sanctity of life. For most of human history the law had leaned on the side that life is worth preserving. That view is now shifting, and we are moving toward the idea that a substantial number of people are better off dead. Some have observed that certain changes and practices in our society related to the rejection of creation have "created a moral climate that is supportive of the move away from a high view of life."[32]

In a dramatic courtroom scene in the television version of Jerome Laurence's *Inherit the Wind,* which was based on the famous Scopes Trial, the lawyer for the defense asks a young student whose teacher had taught him evolution, "Did evolution ever do you any harm?" The lawyer asks the boy about his general health and his ability to play baseball, implying that this belief has in no way damaged the young man. While it is true that such a belief may not affect one's athletic ability, it has in time damaged the entire fabric of our society.

Os Guinness has observed that if man is merely an animal, he may just as well live like one.[33] He states that modern man's view of himself in terms of his moral behavior irretrievably alters his view of reality. "Anything left of contemporary concepts of morality and identity will be reduced to the level of the illusory, and the implications for individuals and for civilization are far-reaching."[34] Twenty-five years ago, Guinness warned that man was headed into a period of alienation, followed by mystification and romanticism. He pointed to Nietzsche's view that man is in an "ontological predicament," like being tied by a rope over an abyss. He is caught in an impossible struggle that results in the great seasickness of a world without God.[35]

It was this concept from Nietzsche that led the French existentialist Jean-Paul Sartre to call his first novel *Nausea*. In it, Sartre concluded that "every existent is born without reason, prolongs itself out of weakness and dies by chance." Thus, Sartre saw life as a fundamental absurdity without God.[36]

When man faces the awfulness of naked *secularism*, Guinness argues, he retreats into a psychological mystification by which he arbitrarily attempts to assign meaning to his life by establishing norms of behavior by the consensus of the population. The end result of this process is the legitimization of one man's abnormality as freedom from another man's normality. An extreme example of this was found in the Soviet Union, when those criticizing society were sent to mental asylums for "paranoid delusions about reforming society."[37] One such accused geneticist, Zhores Medvedev, said, "If things go on like this, it will end with healthy, sane people sitting in mad houses, while dangerous mental cases will walk about freely."[38]

The final stage of the decline of Western thought is *romanticism.* This occurs when we give up the aspirations of a Judeo-Christian world-view and begin to romanticize the consequences. For example, when Judeo-Christian views of death, dying, and eternal life are eliminated, secularists begin romanticizing a pragmatic and casual approach to death as the ultimate escape. Guinness also warned that this would eventually lead to a revival of the concept of reincarnation as modern man's ultimate attempt to escape the meaninglessness of nonbeing.[39]

THE NEW AGE RAGE

Modern man has reached the point at which he does not want to face the logical consequences of a secular world without God. But instead of repenting of his rebellion against God, he is now turning to a kind of *scientific mysticism* that

171

has been popularized as the New Age movement.[40] Modern New Age mysticism is a combination of transcendentalism, spiritualism, oriental mysticism, and transpersonal psychology.[41] It rests upon the humanist psychology that emphasizes the elevation of personal growth as the highest good on the list of man's hierarchical needs.[42]

Twenty-first-century man has come to the ultimate conclusion that he needs hope beyond himself to solve the problems of life. His choices are relatively few indeed. He can turn to God, himself, others, nature, or a mystic collective consciousness. In reality, he only has two choices: himself or God. Ironically, man's rationalism has driven him to irrationality. Either he must accept the logical consequences of living in a world without God or he must turn to God. All other options are merely wishful thinking.

Modern Americans, however, usually find it difficult to throw God away altogether. We always seem to rely on some popular myth that Superman (or someone like him) is going to come from outer space to save the world. Unfortunately, our own scientific rationality ought to tell us this isn't so. The blatant secularist knows it isn't so and has to admit that man must solve his problems alone.

The great cause for despair in Western culture is the stark realization that man may well be closer to destroying himself than to solving his problems. Everyone born after Hiroshima knows the great horror of living in a world that could be destroyed by the very technology that has made it great. This lurks in the subconscious of everyone in our society, representing such an ugly reality that we psychologically suppress it and blank it out. In the meantime, we make nearly every decision in light of that subconscious truth and pretend it isn't so. Fantasy replaces reality and leaves us victims of our own emotions. Before we realize it, we are trapped in spiritual darkness.

8

Religion
of the Future

*In later times some will abandon the faith and follow deceiv-
ing spirits and things taught by demons.*
—1 TIMOTHY 4:1 NIV

THE NEW AGE MOVEMENT IS PART OF THE GREAT
paradigm shift of our times. We are continually moving
from information (objective truth) to emotion (subjective
truth). The appeal to the heart has replaced the intellect of
the mind. This may not be the final form of the new religion, but it is symptomatic of the new way of thinking that
permeates the new millennium. The battle for the heart is
wrapped in the jargon of a mystical spirituality that rejects
objective truth in favor of subjective experience.

The *Harry Potter* phenomenon is clear evidence of this

trend. The record-breaking movies and best-selling books by J. K. Rowling immerse children into a world of witchcraft, wizardry, ghosts, and goblins. Shifting staircases, levitating objects, and slightly loopy ghosts are all presented in good-natured fun while the readers, mostly children, are drawn into a fascination with the occult.

Let's get one thing clear: The New Age movement is not a passing fad. It has been gaining momentum for three decades. It represents a cultural revolt against the spiritual void of secularism. It was not until the late 1980s that the general public became aware of the popular appeal of New Age thinking. Actress Shirley MacLaine's autobiography, *Out on a Limb,* and several subsequent books openly promoted New Age ideals: "I am God," reincarnation, seances, crystals, and pyramid power. In August 1987, twenty thousand New Agers gathered at various "sacred sites" around the world for the Harmonic Convergence, a supposed cosmic event of great significance. By December 7, 1987, the New Age movement had made the cover of *Time* magazine.

And it's gained speed ever since.

New Age thinking is rooted in the counterculture of the 1960s. Though the hippie movement died out after the Vietnam War, its ideas remained. Elliot Miller observes that New Agers are primarily baby boomers (born shortly after World War II) who have recycled, but not rejected, the *ideals* of the hippie counterculture:[1]

1. Antimaterialism

2. Utopianism

3. Exaltation of nature

4. Rejection of traditional morality

5. Fascination with the occult

Miller refers to the New Age subculture as "another America" existing alongside the secular and religious establishments and competing with them for cultural dominance.[2] He characterizes New Agers as sincere, intelligent, optimistic, and humanitarian. Unlike traditional Eastern mystics, New Agers are positive about life and their involvement in the world. They embrace the future while promoting the ideals of global peace, economic prosperity, political unification, and ecological balance.

New Agers have been variously described as "Western mystics," "hippies come of age," "secular prosperity theologians," and "secularized spiritualists." But it is their combination of subjective spirituality and secular morality that leaves them so vulnerable to satanic influence.

AGE OF AQUARIUS

New Age participants hitchhike much of their ideology on the concepts of astrology, especially the idea of the

"Age of Aquarius." They believe that a spiritual age is now upon us in which many people are evolving into advanced stages of spiritual consciousness. They further believe that personal transformation must precede planetary transformation. This means that people involved in the New Age are committed to the proselytization of new converts to their cause. They are out to win people over to what some, like Marilyn Ferguson, have called "the Aquarian conspiracy."[3]

Astrologers believe that human evolution is progressing in cycles corresponding to the signs of the zodiac. Each cycle allegedly lasts about two thousand years. Following the beliefs of astrologers, New Age believers see man moving from the Piscean (intellectual) Age into the Aquarian (spiritual) Age.

Constance Cumbey, a Christian attorney from Detroit, Michigan, first alerted the evangelical community to the New Age menace in her book *The Hidden Dangers of the Rainbow* (1983). While many feel she overreacted to the conspiracy threat from the New Age movement, no one can doubt her sincerity in attempting to alert the Christian public to what she discovered in New Age books, seminars, and lectures. Even Elliot Miller admits, "There is an 'Aquarian Conspiracy'—a conscious effort by a broad-based movement to subvert our cultural establishment so that we might enter a 'New Age' based on mysticism and occultism."[4]

NEW AGE ACTIVISM

Since the publication of Mark Satin's *New Age Politics* in 1978, it has been clear that New Age activists intend to continue promoting a political agenda for a united global community under the control of a one-world government.[5] In order to convince society of the need for this new world order, New Agers have adopted several promotional techniques:

- **Psychic healing.** Using man's inner psychic energy to heal his emotional conflicts and distresses.

- **Holistic health.** Combining diet and inner dynamic force to produce a healthy and productive life.

- **Transpersonal education.** Also called holistic education, it targets public education as the medium to combine humanistic and mystical approaches to learning.

- **Values clarification.** An educational technique that emphasizes that one's values emerge from within one's self and not from external codes, such as the Ten Commandments.

- **Human Potential.** Thought-reform techniques promoting the use of guided imagery and visualization through organization development (O.D.) and organization transformation (O.T.) seminars. Used to bring humanistic psychology and Eastern mysticism into the workplace.

New Agers promote the basic human values as (1) survival, (2) interdependence, (3) autonomy, and (4) humanness. This leaves little or no place for biblical Christianity. In fact, the occult connection with New Age thinking is anti-Christian. A new world order based upon New Age ideology would likely view evangelical Christianity as bigoted, divisive, and sectarian. This could easily set the stage for "justified" persecution of Christians as rebels against the cause of world peace.

NEW AGE SPIRITISM

The gasoline that drives the New Age movement is spiritism, which is the practice of communicating with departed human spirits or extrahuman intelligences through a human medium by the process of channeling. In his recent book, *Channeling*, Joe Klimo claims that channeling involves a human being who is possessed by an external force, power, or personality.[6] This entity exercises control over the perceptual, cognitive, and self-reflective capacities of the person who has relinquished himself to the external force.

If you wonder whether such beliefs have hit mainstream media, consider this: The Disney network currently airs a program called *So Weird* that involves characters who have animal spirit guides. Commercials for the program encourage children to find their own animal spirit guides as well. And the Web site www.zoogdisney.com has links that lead to dark and evil-looking panther eyes. When clicked, a story involving animal spirit guides springs to the screen.

And this is a Web site recommended by hundreds of teachers across the country.

The Bible clearly warns against involvement with witchcraft, seances, and mediums. Deuteronomy 18:10–12 commands, "There shall not be found among you . . . a medium, or a spiritist, or one who calls up the dead. For all who do these things are an abomination to the LORD." The prophet Isaiah warned, "When men tell you to consult mediums and spiritists, who whisper and mutter, should not a people inquire of their God? Why consult the dead on behalf of the living?" (Isaiah 8:19 NIV). Scripture acknowledges the reality of demonic spirits and their attempts to communicate through human mediums (1 Samuel 28:6–14; Acts 16:16–19). It always presents them as evil, deceptive, and malevolent. They are channels to Satan's lies, not to God's truth.

TUNE IN AND BEAM UP

Popular channels in the modern New Age movement vary from those receiving *telepathic* messages (Alice Bailey and

Helen Schucman), *full-trance* channels (Kevin Ryerson and Jack Pursel), and *incarnational* channels (J. Z. Knight and Penny Tores). Each in his or her own way claims to be delivering messages from someone or something beyond this present earthly experience. They are in essence claiming supernatural revelations of truth.

The channeling craze is "like having a telephone to God," Ryerson told Shirley MacLaine. It has caught on because it short-circuits real prayer. It involves little or no disciplined study. And it promises instant answers, inspired advice, quick solutions, and easy access to spiritual information not readily available to others.

In the first chapter of their book *Opening to Channel,* Sanaya Roman and Duane Packer introduce the reader to a welcome message from their channels, Orin and DaBen.[7] This message announces channeling as an evolutionary leap upward into spiritual unfoldment and conscious transformation. Channeling, according to Orin and DaBen, builds a bridge to a loving meaningful higher consciousness known as the All-That-Is (or the Universal Mind).

Roman and Packer promise several benefits from channeling via the message of Orin and DaBen:

• Channeling will give you the wise teacher you seek from within yourself.

- Your guide will be a friend who is always there to support you.

- Channeling will help you learn to love yourself more.

- Spirit guides will help you achieve new levels of personal power and spiritual growth.

- All you have to do is ask for a guide and one will come to you.

Mixing a little bit of scientific information about electromagnetic fields together with self-help psychology and occult spiritism, the seeker is left wide open to buy into the demonic realm of the spirit world. Opening your soul to channeling the psychologically induced impressions of one's so-called spirit guide plays right into the hands of Satan. Such a subjective and self-centered approach to truth leaves one the victim of "the father of lies" (John 8:44).

THE NEW THEOLOGY

C. S. Lewis, in his masterpiece *The Screwtape Letters*, warns against producing a vaguely devotional mood of prayer that requires no real concentration on the will or intelligence. This bears only a superficial resemblance to true prayer: "That is exactly the sort of prayer we want," Screwtape advises Wormwood. The demonic uncle goes on to advise his nephew that the best way to nullify human prayer is to get people to "turn their gaze away from Him (God) toward themselves."[8]

This is precisely the danger in the New Age cults. The objective focus is shifted away from God toward self and results in some of the most incredible self-deception ever perpetrated on the general public: channeling, visualization, astral projection, altered consciousness, reincarnation, and even time travel!

In her book *Creative Visualization*, Shakti Gawain advises her readers to relax into "a deep, quiet, meditative state of mind" in order to visualize the reality that they want to create for themselves. "It is not necessary to have faith in any power outside yourself," she adds.[9] To help her readers find the power of positive affirmation, Gawain suggests they say the following:[10]

- Every day in every way I'm getting better and better.

- My life is blossoming in total perfection.

- Everything I need is already within me.

- I am the master of my life.

- It's okay for me to have everything I want!

Then she explains, "Affirmations are often most powerful and inspiring when they include references to spiritual sources. Mention of God, Christ, Buddha, or any great master adds spiritual energy to your affirmation."[11] She closes with the following examples:

- My higher self is guiding me in everything I do.
- The power of God flows through me.
- Divine love is working through me.
- I am one with my higher nature, and I have infinite creative power.
- Wherever I am, God is, and all is well!

New Age theology represents a do-it-yourself form of religion. A person can pick and choose whatever ideas, beliefs, concepts, and concerns happen to appeal to him personally. The rest can merely be set aside; they need not be rejected.

The bottom line is obvious. New Age theology rests upon pantheism. Its logical paradigm is

> All is God,
> God is all,
> Man is part of all,
> Therefore, man is God.

The only thing separating man from God is his own consciousness, not his sin, New Agers believe. Thus, they propose finding God within oneself by altering one's consciousness through meditation, chanting, channeling, sensory expansion, ecstatic dancing, and even fire walking. The New Age approach to spirituality is more a matter of experience than belief. Altered consciousness leads to self-realization, which results in personal transformation (the New Ager's form of salvation). In this process, personal experience becomes the final authority to define one's spiritual journey.

NEW AGE NETWORK

In his very helpful book *A Crash Course on the New Age Movement*, Elliot Miller defines the New Age movement as an informal network of individuals and organizations bound together by common values (mysticism and monism) and a common vision (coming new age of Aquarius).[12] Within the New Age network are several separate strands that interconnect:

1. **Consciousness movement.** Those advocating the expansion of human consciousness by altered mental states, resulting in the expansion of human awareness.

2. **Holistic health.** Those encouraging better food and diet for better mental and spiritual development.

3. **Human potential.** The self-help psychology of self-awareness, self-actualization, and self-improvement.

4. Eastern mysticism. Various gurus advocating transcendental meditation, astral projection, reincarnation, and various Hindu doctrines that view the material world as illusionary.

5. Occultism. Pseudoscientific return to witchcraft, satanism, shamans, mediums, palm readers, and tarot cards.

The blend of these various elements varies with every individual and every subgroup within the New Age network. Some lean toward ecological issues (save the planet); others lean toward global peace issues (make love, not war); and still others prefer a mystical orientation that mixes meditation, yoga, and astrology with a strong belief in reincarnation. The combinations of any of these elements are like fingers of an intellectual hand reaching out to potential followers.

Miller states, "New Agers tend to be eclectic: they draw what they think is the best from many sources. Long-term exclusive devotion to a single teacher, teaching, or technique is not the norm. They move from one approach to another in their spiritual quests."[13] Because there is no objective truth, the New Age believer creates his or her own subjective truth. Therefore, the uniqueness of the gospel of salvation through Jesus Christ can be easily rejected with, "That's *your* truth, but it's not for me."

It is this merging of scientific mysticism with a rejection of materialistic secularism that has resulted in New Age thinking. This thinking then couples with the Human Potential movement, which offers a number of techniques for advancing one's metaphysical evolution. The New Age transformationalists seek the total transformation of society along ideological lines consistent with their own beliefs. By challenging the "myths" of matter, time, space, and death, people who adhere to New Age thinking believe they will release our untapped human potential to create a new and better world.

The great danger in New Age thinking is its unwillingness to face the facts. There is no scientific proof for the mystical claims of reincarnation, spirit guides, astral projection, time travel, or a dozen other ideas popularized at New Age psychic fairs. When the process of mystification is complete, it leaves man dangling at the end of his own intellectual rope—with nowhere to land!

The spiritual void caused by the rejection of Christianity has left modern man desperately looking for a spiritual reality beyond himself. New Age believers argue that our over-emphasis on rationality has caused us to lose our intuitive awareness. Like the old Jedi warrior in *Star Wars*, New Age participants advise people to let their feelings guide them. The collective "force" of humanity (past and present) will guide you better than following mere objective facts, they teach.

In the end, objectivity is thrown out the window by

New Age believers. In turn, they want to blame the rest of the world for its collective intellectual blindness. This leads to the great *paradigm shift,* or new way of thinking about old problems. Leading the vanguard of New Age thinkers is Fritjof Capra, who argues that the old mechanistic perspective of the world must be replaced by the view that sees the world as one indivisible, dynamic whole whose parts are interrelated in the cosmic process.

SELLING IT TO THE PUBLIC

In order to intellectually promote the idea of a new world order, New Ager proponents turn to mysticism as an ally. Synthesis replaces analysis of scientific data. The intuitive ability to recognize "wholes" replaces the need to analyze all the "parts." Capra states, "The systems view of life is spiritual in its deepest essence and thus consistent with many ideas held in mystical traditions."[14]

New Age believers tie their concepts of an emerging world order to the concept of purposeful and creative evolution. Following the ideas of German philosopher G. W. F. Hegel, they view God as a *process* rather than a person. Thus, for New Age participants, evolution is "God in process." Elliot Miller observes, "Without such faith in evolution, New Age thinkers would be incapable of maintaining their distinctive optimism."[15]

Consequently, people involved in the New Age believe in the evolutionary emergence of a new collective consciousness that will result in a new humanity. They will solve the threats of nuclear war, ecological disaster, and economic collapse by an intuitive and mystical approach to life. New Age thinker Donald Keys put it like this: "A new kind of world—the world into which we are already moving—requires a new kind of person, a person with a planetary perspective."[16]

To make this hopeful human improvement work, New Age teachings propose a quantum leap forward in evolution. John White says, "We are witnessing the final phase of homo sapiens and the simultaneous emergence of what I have named Homo Noeticus, a more advanced form of humanity . . . As we pass from the Age of Ego to the Age of God, civilization will be transformed from top to bottom. A society founded on love and wisdom will emerge."[17]

All of this may seem like wishful thinking in light of the human tragedies of crime, war, drought, and starvation. But to the New Age believer, it is a religion—with faith in evolution as the process and the worship of the planet as God. On this basis, people caught up in the New Age call upon everyone to surrender their personal agendas to the ecological well-being of the living Earth, "Gaia." "Save the planet" is the evangelistic cry of the New Age movement.

It is this kind of mental gymnastics that enables the New Age to redefine the terms and concepts of spirituality.

They are ready to accept the earth or the self as God. They believe in the existence of departed spirits, ghosts, time travelers, extraterrestrial beings, angels, demons, witches, and wizards. Their influence can be seen in movies like *Star Wars, Ghost, Field of Dreams, E.T., Jewel of the Nile,* and *Dances with Wolves.*

The New Agers see great spirituality in Indian medicine men, Hindu gurus, Tibetan lamas, Sufi mystics, Zen teachers, and Oriental hermits. They are united in their rejection of the God of the Bible, the deity of Christ, and the personality of the Holy Spirit. Jesus is repackaged as the cosmic Christ. In a do-it-yourself religion, we ought not be surprised to find a make-your-own Jesus!

Desperately seeking answers to the great human problems of our time, the New Age believer turns to himself, the planet, the forces of nature, and the spirit world for help. But in his quest, he misses the true Christ—the real source of the peace, security, and stability he seeks.

In the meantime, people who follow New Age thinking are left hoping for some great cosmic deliverer to rescue the world and preserve its peace. Constance Cumbey is right when she says, "For the first time in history there is a viable movement—the New Age movement—that truly meets all the scriptural requirements for the antichrist and the political movement that will bring him on the world scene."[18]

The stage has certainly been set for a new world order based upon a subjective view of reality. It will only be a matter of time until the objective standards of truth will be totally eroded in the modern world. We are getting closer, and the only real question left is: How much time do we have until it's too late?

PART THREE

Heart
to
Heart

9

Searching
Our Hearts

Search me, O God, and know my heart.
—*PSALM 139:23*

AS WITH THE CHARACTERS IN THE OPENING SHORT story, the problems of postmodern society are obvious. The signs of spiritual emptiness are everywhere. People give up easily, and then hope for answers that can never be found aside from God.

The only solution is for us to search our hearts and turn to the Lord for help. The Bible tells us, "If My people who are called by My name will humble themselves, and pray and seek My face, and turn from their wicked ways, then I will hear from heaven, and will forgive their sin and heal their land"(2 Chronicles 7:14). While this promise was initially given to the Old Testament people of Israel, it certainly reflects the heart of God for His people in every generation.

We need a genuine revival of true spirituality. Revival has always been the method by which God has moved His people to awaken society to see its need for a personal relationship with Him. When our hearts are moved to see our own spiritual need, then God will use us to speak to the needs of a world that is lost and hopeless without Him. But genuine revival can only begin when we confess our sins and turn our hearts toward God.

The answer for the spiritual vacuum of our times is a vital spiritual relationship with God. Most people are aware of their spiritual needs. They feel the emptiness of their souls every day. They want something to fill that void, but they don't know how to find it. That is why the message of the Bible is so important. It tells us how to have a personal, spiritual relationship with God. It assures us that God loves us and sent His son, Jesus Christ, to die for our sins so that we might experience the grace and forgiveness of God (John 3:16).

Christians call this experience salvation. It begins the moment we place our faith in Jesus Christ as our personal Lord and Savior. That is the first step on our spiritual journey. We are born again by the power of God's Spirit activating our dead hearts with spiritual life. Suddenly, we who were dead are made spiritually alive in Christ.

What is spirituality? It certainly is not an emotional feeling that transports us into a mystical relationship with God. It is a state of being that takes time for the Holy Spirit to develop in the human heart. You can be saved in an instant and raptured in a "twinkling of an eye," but it takes a lifetime to become a spiritual person.

A new Christian may experience momentary spiritual "highs," but only a mature Christian will develop long term in the sense of true spirituality. Paul must have had that in mind when he told the Corinthians, "And I, brethren, could not speak to you as to spiritual people but as to carnal, as to babes in Christ" (1 Corinthians 3:1). These Corinthian Christians were babies because they were still carnal. They had not matured or grown up spiritually. They were saved, but they were factious, critical, contentious, and had other problems not associated with a truly spiritual person. Paul had spent a great deal of time in Corinth with these people, but they had not abandoned the influence of the Greek world around them. Consequently they were baby Christians—even long after they should have been mature.

We should be careful not to confuse true spirituality and seniority. As a pastor for over thirty years, I (Tim) know all too well the problem the local church gets itself into when it elects people to its boards and committees on the basis of seniority rather than spiritual maturity. Just because a person is an active tithing man of a congregation does not make him qualified for service on the deacon board—or to be the pastor of the church. Seniority may qualify you for retirement, but it does not make you a spiritually mature person.

By contrast, you don't have to wait a decade to be a spiritually mature person. Most of the early Christian leaders were active leaders before they had been saved more than five to ten years. We see the same thing today. We have four-year Christians who are far more spiritually mature than some who have spent fifty years merely attending church.

A spiritually mature Christian is one who is controlled by the Holy Spirit (Ephesians 5:18) and manifests the nine fruits of the Spirit (Galatians 5:22–23), who walks in holiness, who knows the Word of God, and who diligently seeks to do His will because he loves Him (John 14:21). While that does take time, it does not take a lifetime. The apostle Paul spent three years in Arabia after his conversion before Barnabas brought him up to Antioch to begin serving as an elder. By this time he was spiritually mature enough to take a position as a teacher of the Word. Several years later he became a leader in his own right. But this was a gradual process.

Although it is impossible to say when a person becomes spiritually mature, I think we can gain insight from 1 John 2:12–14 where we find three stages of growth compared to the spiritual life: "little children," "young men," and "fathers."

A spiritual child is one who is newly born again. While salvation is a free gift, spiritual growth is the result of growing in grace and the knowledge of our Lord through study of His Word and faith. A newborn "babe," as Peter calls him, or a "little child" as John labels him, is not going to be a victorious Christian most of the time. He may experience an up-and-down life spiritually for a time until his commitment to the Word makes him an overcomer. At that point, he is a "young man" in Christ; that is, he overcomes the "wicked one" by "the word of God [which] abides in you" more often than he is overcome. Note the gradual growth process. Finally, as this person continues studying the Word, walking in the Spirit and in obedience to the Word, he believes such a faith is based on knowing God, and becomes a father of the faith. One thing about spiritual fathers—they spiritually reproduce themselves in other people. Being conformed to our Lord's image will make us like Christ. As He served the Father by seeking that which was lost, so will we. As His heart reached out to those in need, so will ours. Spiritual maturity is developing a heart like Christ's heart.

In this day of instant everything, we need to understand that there are no shortcuts to maturity—physical or spiritual. There is, however, one major difference between physical maturity and spiritual maturity—*you*. In the physical it is almost automatic. If you eat three meals a day and get a reasonable amount of exercise and rest, you will gradually mature into adulthood. Spiritually, it depends on *you*. God is for you, the Holy Spirit is available to you, and you have the Word to guide you. How fast you grow depends on how long it takes you to learn the principles, wisdom, and knowledge of God found in His Word and to incorporate these into your daily life.

1. Bible Study

One thing is certain—there is no such thing as spiritual maturity without Bible study. It may come through hearing the Bible in church, TV, cassettes, Bible school, or through reading and studying the Word for yourself. But just as you can't grow physically without food, you can't grow spiritually without the spiritual food of the Word of God. That may be why the Bible refers to itself as milk, bread, and meat.

The success of your spiritual life is dependent on the effectiveness of your personal Bible study, not your emotions. However, your emotions will influence your Bible study habits just as surely as they influence your physical eating habits.

2. Prayer

Prayer is as essential to a Christian's spiritual life as breathing is to his physical life. All Christians pray. How they pray, however, is almost as varied as people. Some people never develop a deep or disciplined prayer life because they have never seen one modeled for them. How you pray will influence how others pray.

The Bible is filled with teaching, commands, and instructions on prayer—from "pray without ceasing" to ". . . let your requests be made known to God." There are hundreds of promises regarding prayer. It seems to be God's means of blessing His children and supplying their needs. If you haven't done a Bible study on prayer, you should, and you will find a wealth of material to work with.

But it isn't just formal instruction in the Word that gives you your instructions on prayer. Your pastor-teacher or the individual God sends you to instruct you in His ways will have a profound influence on your prayer life. For instance, prayer patterns will become a model for your own. When you observe the prayer life of a Christian you admire, you are often prone to consider his prayer life to be the secret to his spiritual life. And that is, generally speaking, not true. His prayer life is the result of his instruction, role model, spiritual life, and his temperament. We may not all pray alike but we can all learn the discipline of prayer.

3. Living by Faith

Many years ago I (Tim) came to an interesting observation in my Christian life, and today I have seen nothing that would cause me to change my mind. Very simply, it is this: Faith is more important than intelligence or talent.

I came to this conclusion in answering the question, Why does God seem to use some people more than others? I think that it is a very legitimate question, as is the second that bears on it—Why does God use some very ordinary people more than some of the more talented and intelligent? Now that does not mean God does not use gifted people. The apostle Paul was obviously a brilliant man with the best education available in his day, and God used him mightily. Yet he also used Peter, James, and John, who were ordinary and "unlearned men." I have seen the same thing in churches I have served. I have seen God use both brilliant scholars and people with very average talent and low IQ. I have seen Him seem to bypass some brilliant Christians as well as ordinary saints.

Then I discovered the common denominator. God is no respecter of persons—He uses anyone, from Balaam's ass to the wisest man who ever lived or who ever will live. What is that common denominator? *Faith.* God Himself said, "Without faith it is impossible to please [God]" (Hebrews 11:6). The one thing that raises one Christian above another is not looks, brains, talent, or even opportunity; it is faith. 2 Chronicles 16:9 tells us that "the eyes of the LORD range throughout the earth, to strengthen those whose hearts are fully committed to him" (NIV). In this context, "fully committed" means "full of faith." God's eyes are continually running up and down the earth looking for men and women of faith. The New Testament tells us that the one thing God requires in us is *faithfulness* (Matthew 25:21).

We have already seen that faith comes through the Word of God. It also comes through the Holy Spirit, for it is one of the nine fruits or results of the Spirit according to Galatians 5:22. But there is another way the gift of faith comes into our lives—from one step of faith to another step of faith (Romans 1:17). That is, as we take one step of faith, it stretches our faith for the next step. People who never trust God for the first step of faith will never become strong in faith, and God will not use them very much—regardless of how much natural ability they might have.

The apostle Peter is often ridiculed by preachers and Bible teachers for sinking as he walked on the water to Jesus. The truth is, of all the disciples, he was the only one with sufficient faith to walk on water. To this day that feat has only been accomplished by our Lord and Peter. What made the difference—bigger feet? More intelligence? Of course not—faith made the difference. At a moment in time, Peter had more faith than the other disciples, and he walked on water.

Are there opportunities you have passed up due to lack of faith? Probably! Most of us have. That's why you should develop your faith through regular study of the Word and walk in the control of the Spirit, being obedient to all you know God wants you to do. Take that step of faith. Be sure of this. No one takes giant steps of faith who has not already taken baby steps. God leads us from faith to faith.

4. Personal Holiness

We live in an unholy age. And unfortunately we do not hear much about the holiness God requires of Christians. That is why so much immorality, carnality, and worldliness is creeping into our churches today. Be sure of this—no one will be spiritually mature who does not practice mental holiness, and today you will have to work at it. The best place to start is to examine what the Bible says on the subject. Consider the following:

Be holy for I am holy. (1 Peter 1:16)

Make every effort to live in peace with all men and to be holy; without holiness no one will see the Lord. (Hebrews 12:14 NIV)

Since everything will be destroyed . . . what kind of people ought you to be? You ought to live holy and godly lives . . . (2 Peter 3:11 NIV)

Since we have these promises, dear friends, let us purify ourselves from everything that contaminates body and spirit, perfecting holiness out of reverence for God. (2 Corinthians 7:1 NIV)

Holiness is not easy, but it is essential. And like faith, little steps lead to bigger steps—in either direction. And your emotions are no help! Men are especially vulnerable in this regard. Our Lord taught men not to look at women in lust. In so doing, he established the male Christian's principal source of temptation. Godly men, regardless of their emotions, have learned to look at women without lusting. Jesus did not say a man could not look at women. It is looking and lusting that is sin. A godly man will learn to look on women admiringly, as he can legitimately look on any beautiful object with approval. But it takes mental discipline and spiritual determination to learn to recognize the line between looking and lusting and to refuse to cross it.

The best scriptural challenge in this regard is 2 Corinthians 10:5; practice it throughout your entire life:

Casting down imaginations, and every high thing that exalteth itself against the knowledge of God, and bringing into captivity every thought to the obedience of Christ. (KJV)

FACING AFFLICTIONS

Everyone has afflictions in life—even Spirit-controlled Christians. Our Lord, who was perfect and sinless, and on whom the spirit rested without measure, was afflicted, grieved, and sorrowed. As you know, He even wept! Job, one of the godliest men who ever lived, suffered the premature death of his children, the loss of his cattle and goods, and even attack on his health as a testimony to man and Satan that God is able to supply the needs of the afflicted saint.

You too will suffer affliction, if you have not already. Sickness and death are a part of life. Insult, injury, and rejection are common to all men, and Christians are not exempt. And your first reaction will often be the result of your emotions. At first, your heart will want to react selfishly, but the Holy Spirit within you will restrain that reaction and challenge you to respond in a Christlike manner.

Since most of our human reactions are wrong, what are we to do? Heed the words of Scripture: "Consider it pure joy . . . whenever you face trials [afflictions] of many kinds" (James 1:2 NIV). Instead of reacting in the flesh, react in the Spirit by learning to praise the Lord *in* the circumstances. Not *for* them, but *in* them. There is a difference! There are some circumstances in life for which we cannot give thanks or "consider it pure joy." But there are no circumstances in which we Christians cannot count it all joy or give thanks for God and what He is able to do in the midst of our affliction. The key is the direction of our look. If we look only at the problem, which is normal, we will respond according to our emotions. If, however, we look to God, we will respond according to the scriptural power within us.

THE BOTTOM LINE

Many Christians think they are spiritual, but clearly they are not. Some don't understand what a spiritual Christian is. Others are merely kidding themselves, thinking they are spiritual because they go to church regularly, tithe, and are faithful marriage partners.

A truly spiritual person will do all these things and many more. But the most obvious difference is this: He will walk in the control of the Holy Spirit and thus fulfill the will of God (Ephesians 5:17–18; Galatians 5:16–18).

The bottom line to spirituality will be heart-centered. Who controls your heart? Who uses your body? That's what this life is about. Who controls you—God or Satan? A truly spiritual person dedicates his life to God for whatever use the heavenly Father wishes. In this way he allows God to make him a "living sacrifice" or a living vessel of service (Romans 12:1–2).

He will do all the things mentioned above, including living his life under the control of the Holy Spirit, obedient to whatever God tells him to do. He will not grieve or quench the Spirit (Ephesians 4:30–32; 1 Thessalonians 5:19) by indulging his naturally inherited weaknesses, but will so seek the kingdom of God (Matthew 6:33) that his life will be available to do whatever the Lord commands. His mind will be so renewed by the Holy Spirit through the Word of

God that he will not conform to the paths of this world. And be sure of this: He or she *will be holy*. *True* spirituality will always come clothed in holiness as a result of being filled with the Spirit.

10

A Prescription
for the Heart

And do not be drunk with wine, ...
but be filled with the Spirit.
—*EPHESIANS 5:18*

THE MOST IMPORTANT THING IN THE LIFE OF
any Christian is to be filled with the Holy Spirit. The Lord
Jesus said, "Without Me you can do nothing" (John 15:5).
Christ is in believers in the person of His Holy Spirit.
Therefore our hearts must be soaked, drenched, and saturated in the living Spirit of God. If we are filled with His
spirit, He works fruitfully through us. If we are not filled
with the Holy Spirit, we are unproductive.

It is almost impossible to exaggerate how dependent we
are on the Holy Spirit. We are dependent on Him for

convicting us of sin before and after our salvation, for giving us understanding of the gospel, for bringing us into His kingdom, for empowering us to witness, for guiding us in our prayer lives—in fact, for everything. It is no wonder that evil spirits have tried to counterfeit and confuse the work of the Holy Spirit.

There is probably no biblical subject on which there is more confusion today than that of being filled with the Holy Spirit. Many fine Christian people equate the filling of the Holy Spirit with some emotionally ecstatic experience. Others, because of the excesses of some, have all but eliminated the teaching of the filling of the Holy Spirit. They just do not recognize His importance in their lives.

Satan places two obstacles before mankind: (1) He tries to keep people from receiving Christ as Savior; (2) if he fails in this, he tries to keep Christians from understanding the importance and work of the Holy Spirit. Once a person is converted, Satan seems to have two different approaches. He tries to get us to associate the filling of the Holy Spirit with emotional excesses or—the opposite swing of the pendulum—to ignore the Holy Spirit altogether.

One of the false impressions gained from people is that there is some special "feeling" when one is filled with the Holy Spirit. Before we examine how to be filled with the Holy Spirit, let's see what the Bible says we can expect when we are filled with the Spirit.

WHAT TO EXPECT
WHEN FILLED WITH THE SPIRIT

The Bible teaches that we can expect certain things when we are filled with the Holy Spirit. Galatians 5:22–23 NIV lists nine characteristics of a Spirit-filled life: love, joy, peace, patience, kindness, goodness, faithfulness, gentleness, and self-control. Any individual who is filled with the Holy Spirit is going to manifest these characteristics. Spirit-filled believers do not have to try to manufacture these characteristics or play a part or act out a role to do this. When the Holy Spirit has control of us, we will simply be different than our normal selves.

Many who claim to have had the "filling" or, as some call it, "the anointing," know nothing of love, joy, peace, long-suffering (patience), gentleness, goodness, faithfulness, meekness (kindness), or self-control. But the Bible is clear. These remain the hallmark of the person filled with the Holy Spirit. No matter what one's emotional experience may be, a life devoid of these qualities is a life not filled with the Spirit.

One of the reasons today's generation is looking in all the wrong places for hope and meaning is because they have missed the only One who can fill them with the very qualities they need to satisfy their hearts.

A JOYFUL HEART

Ephesians 5:18–21 says that when the Holy Spirit fills the life of a believer, the Spirit will cause that person to have a singing, thanks-giving heart and a submissive spirit:

> And do not be drunk with wine, in which is dissipation; but be filled with the Spirit, speaking to one another in psalms and hymns and spiritual songs, singing and making melody in your heart to the Lord, giving thanks always for all things to God the Father in the name of our Lord Jesus Christ, submitting to one another in the fear of God.

A singing, thanks-giving heart and a submissive spirit, independent of circumstances, are so unnatural that they can only be ours through the filling of the Holy Spirit. The Spirit of God is able to change the gloomy heart into a song-filled, thankful heart. He is also able to solve our natural rebellion by increasing our faith to the point that we really believe the best way to live is in submission to the will of God.

These results of the Spirit-filled life are also the results of the Word-filled life, as found in Colossians 3:16–18:

> Let the word of Christ dwell in you richly in all wisdom, teaching and admonishing one another in psalms and

hymns and spiritual songs, singing with grace in your hearts to the Lord. And whatever you do in word or deed, do all in the name of the Lord Jesus, giving thanks to God the Father through Him. Wives, submit to your own husbands, as is fitting in the Lord.

It is no accident that the results of the Spirit-filled life (Ephesians 5:18–21) and those of the Word-filled life are one and the same. The Lord Jesus called the Holy Spirit "the Spirit of truth" (John 16:13), and He also said of the Word of God, "Your word is truth" (John 17:17). Why does the Word-filled life cause the same results as the Spirit-filled life? Because the Holy Spirit is the author of the Word of God.

This highlights the error of those who try to receive the Holy Spirit through a once-for-all experience rather than seeing the Spirit-filled life as an intimate relationship with God—described by Jesus as "abiding in Me" (see John 15:4). This relationship is possible as God communes with the Christian and fills the believer's life through the "Word of truth" and as the Christian communes with God in prayer guided by the "Spirit of truth." The conclusion that we can clearly draw here is that the Christian who is Spirit-filled will be Word-filled, and the Word-filled Christian who obeys the Spirit will be Spirit-filled.

THE POWER TO WITNESS

The last thing Jesus told His disciples before ascending into heaven was this: "But you shall receive power when the Holy Spirit has come upon you; and you shall be witnesses to Me in Jerusalem, and in all Judea and Samaria, and to the end of the earth" (Acts 1:8).

Before His crucifixion, Jesus had told them, "Nevertheless I tell you the truth. It is to your advantage that I go away; for if I do not go away, the Helper [Holy Spirit] will not come to you; but if I depart, I will send Him to you" (John 16:7).

Even though the disciples had spent three years with Jesus personally, had heard His messages several times, and were the best-trained witnesses He had, He still instructed them "not to depart from Jerusalem, but to wait for the Promise of the Father"—the Holy Spirit (Acts 1:4). All of their training obviously was incapable of producing results without the power of the Holy Spirit. When the Holy Spirit came on the Day of Pentecost, the disciples witnessed in His power, and three thousand people were saved.

We too can expect to have power to witness when filled with the Holy Spirit. The real evidence of His filling will be demonstrated in others coming to faith in Jesus Christ as their Savior.

The power to witness in the Holy Spirit is not always

discernible. It must be accepted by faith. If we have met the conditions for the filling of the Holy Spirit and then step out and witness for Christ, we should believe we give that witness in the power of the Spirit whether or not we see immediate results. Because the Holy Spirit demonstrated His presence on the Day of Pentecost so dramatically and because occasionally we see the evidence of the Holy Spirit in our lives, we come to think that it should always be obvious, but that is not true. You see, in the sovereign plan of God He has chosen never to violate the right of man's free choice. That means we can witness to someone in the power of the Holy Spirit, and that person might still reject the Savior. We cannot always equate success in witnessing with the power to witness!

One day it was my privilege to witness to an eighty-year-old man. Because of his age and particular problems, I (Tim) made a special effort to meet the conditions of being filled with the Holy Spirit before I went to his home. He paid very close attention as I presented the gospel. When I finished and asked if he would like to receive Christ right then, he said, "No, I'm not ready yet."

I went away amazed that a man his age could say he was "not ready yet." I concluded that I did not witness in the power of the Holy Spirit. My heart was heavy because I thought I had failed.

A short time later I went back to see the man and found

that he had passed his eighty-first birthday. Once again I started to present the gospel to him, but he informed me that he had already received Christ. He had restudied the booklet that I left with him. Alone in his room, he had gotten down on his knees and invited Christ into his life as Savior and Lord. The Spirit had been at work, regardless of what felt like failure to me.

A Christian life filled with the Holy Spirit will produce fruit. What Jesus referred to as "abide in Me" and what the Bible teaches about being "filled with the Spirit" (Ephesians 5:18) are one and the same. Jesus said, "Abide in Me, and I in you. As the branch cannot bear fruit of itself, unless it abides in the vine, neither can you, unless you abide in Me" (John 15:4). This indicates that the abiding life or the Spirit-filled life will produce fruit. If you meet the conditions for the filling of the Holy Spirit, then believe, not by results or sight or feeling, but by faith, that God is working through you to accomplish supernatural results.

GLORIFYING GOD

The Holy Spirit directs us to glorify God and Jesus Christ. Ironically, He does not call attention to Himself. Rather, He points us to the Father and the Son. Notice what Jesus Himself said about the Holy Spirit.

However, when He, the Spirit of truth, has come, He will guide you into all truth; for He will not speak on His own authority, but whatever He hears He will speak; and He will tell you things to come. He will glorify Me [Jesus], for He will take of what is Mine and declare it to you. (John 16:13–14)

A fundamental principle should always be kept in mind regarding the work of the Holy Spirit: He does not glorify Himself, but the Lord Jesus Christ. Anytime anyone but the Lord Jesus receives the glory, you can be sure that what is done is not done in the power of the Holy Spirit, for His express work is to glorify Jesus. This test should always be given to any work that claims to be the work of God's Holy Spirit.

The late F. B. Meyer told the story of a missionary who came to him at a Bible conference after he had spoken on the subject of how to be filled with the Holy Spirit. She confessed that she had never consciously been filled with the Holy Spirit, and was going to go up to the prayer chapel to spend the day searching her soul to see if she could receive His filling.

Later that evening she came back just as Meyer was leaving the auditorium. He asked, "How was it, Sister?" and she said, "I'm not quite sure." He then inquired of her day's activities. She explained that she had read the Word, prayed, confessed her sins, and asked for the filling of the Holy Spirit. She then stated, "I do not feel filled with the Holy Spirit."

Meyer asked, "Tell me, Sister, how is it between you and the Lord Jesus?"

Her face lit up, and with a smile she answered, "Oh, Dr. Meyer, I have never had a more blessed time of fellowship with the Lord Jesus in all of my life."

He replied, "Sister, that is the Holy Spirit."

The Holy Spirit will always make the believer more conscious of Jesus than of Himself.

WHAT ABOUT CHANGE?

People may claim to be "filled with the Spirit," but those who know them best know they are disagreeable, emotionally unstable, or difficult to live with. They have been kidding themselves about being filled with the Spirit. Such behavior is not caused by the Holy Spirit, but by the hardness of their own hearts.

Others who claim to have had some kind of "experience" with the Holy Spirit negate their claim by continuing to manifest the works of the flesh, such as anger, jealousy, and worry. They fail to see that the Holy Spirit wants to change their emotions!

People truly filled with the Spirit will show it by their behavior. The best way to clarify the term *Spirit-filled* is to point out that its basic meaning is "control." A person filled is a person controlled not by themselves but by God.

In Ephesians 5:18, the "filling" is compared negatively to someone who is controlled by alcohol. "Do not be drunk with wine, in which is dissipation [excess]; but be filled with the Spirit." The importance of this verse cannot be exaggerated. It is the most powerful command in the Bible to be "filled" or controlled by the Holy Spirit. Look again at the context. A drunk person is "filled" with wine (alcohol or drugs) when controlled by the substance. The person isn't literally filled with the liquid or the drug (it may take only a small capsule of dust), but if the substance "controls" him, it will alter his behavior—mentally, emotionally, and physically.

There is a point here. God wants us to know something very clearly. Instead of being filled with a mindless substance that controls our behavior, we should be filled with or controlled by the Spirit—meaning that the Spirit will control our behavior. We see this when our weaknesses are controlled by the Holy Spirit, and we act like "new creatures" in Christ.

When an angry, selfish, caustic person becomes kind and compassionate, that is an evidence of the Holy Spirit. When an inconsistent, weak-willed person becomes a person of strong character, that is the control of the Holy Spirit. When a naturally critical, ungrateful person becomes thankful and full of praise, that is the control of the Spirit. When a selfish, stingy, unmotivated person gives both self and possessions to God to serve other people, that is the Holy Spirit.

You can't have the power of God directing your life and act the same way you did when you were controlled by your natural temperament, which is the flesh. Will you be taller, smarter, more talented, or better looking? Not at all! But you will act *differently* because you are now under emotional control. Your heart is being controlled by the Holy Spirit.

What you are emotionally is what you are! If you are out of emotional control, you are out of control. When the Holy Spirit controls your life, you will be dominated by love, joy, peace, long-suffering, gentleness, goodness, faith, meekness, and temperance—not your natural emotions of anger, selfishness, fear, depression, and so forth. In essence, your behavior indicates whether you are filled with the Spirit.

A good test of whether you are filled with the Spirit is how you act under pressure. When Paul and Silas were put in prison for preaching the gospel, they exhibited the filling of the Spirit by rejoicing and singing. That is unnatural! And it is evidence of the Spirit-filled life. When you face the trials and pressures of life with love, joy, peace, thanksgiving, and rejoicing, that can only be one thing at work: the Holy Spirit within you.

This is particularly true in the home, for what we are at home is what we really are. Some people place great emphasis on speaking in tongues or healing or other "works for God" as evidences of being filled with the Holy Spirit. A better test would be to ask a person's partner—or children or neighbors—how that person acts at home.

Why should we place the real test of the Spirit-controlled life at home? Because that is where the Bible places it. Ephesians 5:18 is also the introduction to the longest passage in the New Testament on family living—giving instructions on how wives should treat husbands, how husbands should treat wives and children, and how children should obey and honor their parents.

The conclusion is simple: If you are not controlled by the Holy Spirit at home, you are not controlled by the Spirit. That doesn't mean we cannot exhibit the Spirit-controlled life at church, work, and other places, but we need to begin at home. You see, if we can live the Spirit-filled life at home, we can live it anywhere.

Which brings us to the most important subject of all—how to be filled with the Spirit.

HOW TO BE FILLED WITH THE HOLY SPIRIT

1. Examine Your Life

The Christian interested in the filling of the Holy Spirit must regularly "take heed to" himself (Acts 20:28) or "examine himself" (1 Corinthians 11:28). This self-examination is not to see if we measure up to the standards of other people or the traditions and requirements of the church, but to see if we measure up to the evidence of being filled with the Holy Spirit.

Do we glorify Jesus? Do we have power to witness? Do we lack a joyful, submissive spirit or the nine temperament traits of the Holy Spirit? This self-examination will reveal those areas in which we are deficient and will uncover the sin that causes them.

We cannot be filled with sin and the Holy Spirit at the same time. Sin keeps us from being filled, and our patterns of sin usually follow the attitudes of our hearts. Some may be angry because they are guilty of sexual sin. Others may be angry because they are self-willed and controlling. Some are prone to be critical and fearful, while others may be worrisome, selfish, or stubborn. These are only some of the many sins that can keep us from being filled with the Holy Spirit.

2. Confess All Known Sin

"If we confess our sins, He is faithful and just to forgive us our sins and to cleanse us from all unrighteousness" (1 John 1:9).

The Bible does not put an evaluation on one sin over another, but judges all sin alike. After examining ourselves in the light of the Word of God, we should confess all sin brought to mind by the Holy Spirit, including those characteristics of the Spirit-filled life that we lack.

Our lack of compassion, lack of self-control, lack of humility, lack of gentleness, lack of kindness, and especially our lack of faith all stand as roadblocks on the path to a Spirit-filled life. It's time to confess them and anything else that stands in the way.

God is incredibly merciful. The moment we recognize these deficiencies as sin and confess them to God, He will "cleanse us from all unrighteousness." Until we have done this, we cannot have the filling of the Holy Sprit, for He fills only clean vessels (see 2 Timothy 2:21).

3. Submit Yourself Completely to God

> Likewise you also, reckon yourselves to be dead indeed to sin, but alive to God in Christ Jesus our Lord. Therefore do not let sin reign in your mortal body, that you should obey it in its lusts. And do not present your members as instruments of unrighteousness to sin, but present your-selves to God as being alive from the dead, and your members as instruments of righteousness to God. (Romans 6:11–13)

To be filled with the Holy Spirit, we must make our-selves completely available to God to do anything the Holy Spirit directs us to do. If there is anything in our lives that we are unwilling to do or to be, then we are resisting God, and this always limits God's Spirit! Do not make the mistake of being afraid to give yourself to God!

Romans 8:32 says, "He who did not spare His own Son, but delivered Him up for us all, how shall He not with Him also freely give us all things?" If God loved us so much as to give His Son to die for us, certainly He is interested in nothing but our good; that means we can trust Him with our life. You will never find a miserable Christian in the center of the will of God; God will always accompany His directions with an appetite and desire to do His will.

Resisting the Lord through rebellion stifles the filling of the Spirit. Israel limited the Lord, not only through unbelief, but as Psalm 78:8 says, by becoming "a stubborn and rebellious generation, a generation that did not set its heart aright, and whose spirit was not faithful to God." All resistance to the will of God will keep us from being filled with the Holy Spirit. To be filled with His Spirit, we must yield ourselves to His Spirit just as a man yields Himself to wine for its filling.

For consecrated Christians, giving the Lord control or dominance is often the most difficult thing to do. You see, we can always find some worthy purpose for our lives yet not realize that we are doing good while being filled with ourselves rather than with the Holy Spirit.

At a high-school and college camp, I (Tim) heard an unforgettable testimony from a ministerial student who said that he finally realized what it meant to be filled with the Holy Spirit. As far as he knew, he had not been guilty of the usual sins of the carnal Christian. Actually, he had only one area of resistance in his life. He loved to preach, and the possibilities of being a pastor appealed to him very much, but he did not want the Lord to ask him to be a foreign missionary.

During that week, the Holy Spirit spoke to the young man about that very vocation. When he submitted everything to the Lord and said, "Yes, I'll go to the ends of the earth," for the first time he experienced the true filling of the Holy Spirit. Months later he admitted, "I don't believe the Lord wants me to be a missionary after all; He just wanted me to be *willing* to be a missionary."

When you give your life to God, do not attach any strings or conditions to it. He is such a God of love that you can safely give yourself without reservation, knowing that His plan and use of your life will be far better than yours. And, remember, the attitude of a yielded heart is absolutely necessary for the filling of God's Spirit. Your will is the will of the flesh, and the Bible says that "the flesh profits nothing" (John 6:63).

THE SIX BIG QUESTIONS

Much of your life's outcome will be decided by your answers to the following six questions:

1. Where shall I go for training after high school?

2. What vocation should I pursue?

3. Whom shall I marry?

4. Where shall I live?

5. For whom shall I work?

6. Which church shall I attend?

A Spirit-filled Christian will be sensitive to the Spirit's leading not only in answering these big questions, but the smaller ones as well. I have observed that many Christians who have made the right decisions on life's six big questions are still not filled with the Spirit because they are not totally yielded to the Spirit of God.

Someone has suggested that being yielded to the Spirit is being available to the Spirit. Peter and John in Acts 3 make a good example of that. They were on their way to the temple to pray when they saw a lame man begging alms. Because they were sensitive to the Holy Spirit, they healed him "in the name of Jesus Christ of Nazareth." The man began leaping about, praising God until a crowd gathered. Peter, still sensitive to the Holy Spirit, began preaching, and "many of those who heard the word believed; and the number of the men came to be about five thousand" (Acts 4:4).

I fear we are often so engrossed in some good Christian

activity that we are not "available" when the Spirit leads. Many a Christian has said no to the Holy Spirit when offered an opportunity to teach Sunday school.

"Lord, here am I; use me," many Christians say. But when asked to teach or make calls or witness, we are too busy painting, golfing, or pursuing happiness. What is the problem? That person simply isn't available to the Spirit.

Remember this point: A Christian yielded to God takes time to do what the Spirit directs.

Let me warn you that Christians who are interested enough in the Spirit-filled life to read a book like this may yet miss His filling, even if only by a fraction of an inch. Most Christians are basically committed to Christ, but all of us are tempted to hold some area back from God.

A hobby, a habit, a person, a pet sin. Any of these and other distractions can keep us from being filled with the Spirit. We may rationalize and say, "I am *almost* completely yielded to God. Why doesn't He accept that?"

But our God is a jealous God.

He will not share your affection with another. He wants your whole heart. You find that in the first commandment to "have no other gods before Me" (Exodus 20:3). Our Lord reiterated that in the New Testament when He said, "You shall love the LORD your God with all your heart, with all your soul, with all your strength, and with all your mind" (Luke 10:27). This is the most important key to being filled with His Spirit—total, unconditional yieldedness to Him. Not 98.4 percent, but 100 percent!

Don't worry. You will never be sorry. We have never known anyone who ever yielded completely to God who lived to regret it. He wants to bless your life. But He won't do it until you first yield everything to Him. The best bargain we ever made was in giving ourselves totally, unconditionally to Him to do with us anything He sees fit. That was over forty years ago for both of us, and we reap the dividends from those decisions every day. Don't cheat yourself out of unlimited blessing by holding back anything from God. It isn't worth it.

Some years ago a doctor named Ralph, the chief surgeon at a major hospital in Los Angeles, shared with me (Tim) how he had experienced the Spirit-filled life years before. It seemed that when he finished medical school, he had a problem. He wanted to specialize in three things: surgery, research, and teaching. The medical counselors admitted he was qualified to do any one of the three, but could only choose one. "In medicine you can only specialize in one area," they said. So he prayed that the Lord would have one of those specialty schools invite him to study; the open door would indicate God's leading.

Instead, he was invited by all three schools, which didn't solve his problem. So he joined the marines! That did, of course, solve his problem for three years. But one night, out in the South Pacific after his tour of duty, he was faced with the same decision. The next day he would fly back to the United States to pick up the pieces of his medical career. What path would he take? Kneeling in the sand under a palm tree, he cried out to God, "Heavenly Father, I know You have something special for me to do. Whatever it is, I just want You to know, I'm Your boy!"

As Ralph, now forty-eight years old, told me this story, I saw hot tears in his eyes and a smile on his face. He said, "Tim, do you know what I do for a living? I spend one-third of my time in surgery, one-third in research, and one-third in teaching—just what they told me I couldn't do!"

I was looking into the face of a very fulfilled man. Why? Because he was so smart? Not really. It was because he had given his life to God. He admitted, "That was the best bargain I ever made."

And so it will be for you if you give yourself without reservation to God.

4. Ask to Be Filled with the Holy Spirit

"If you then, being evil, know how to give good gifts to your children, how much more will your heavenly Father give the Holy Spirit to those who ask Him!" (Luke 11:13).

When Christians have examined themselves, confessed all known sin, and yielded themselves without reservation to God, they are then ready to receive the filling of the Spirit of God. How? By asking to be filled with the Spirit. Any suggestion to present-day believers to first wait or tarry or labor or suffer is man's suggestion. Only the disciples were told to wait, and that was because the Holy Spirit had not yet come on the Day of Pentecost. Since that day, God's children have only to ask for His filling to experience it.

The Lord Jesus compares God's answer to our request with our treatment of our earthly children. Certainly a good father would not make his children beg for something he commanded them to have. How much less does God make us beg to be filled with the Holy Spirit—which He has commanded. It is just as simple as that. Remember, God is more interested in filling us than we are in being filled.

But don't forget this next, fifth, step.

5. Believe You Are Filled with the Spirit

"But he who doubts is condemned if he eats, because he does not eat from faith; for whatever is not from faith is sin" (Romans 14:23).

"In everything give thanks; for this is the will of God in Christ Jesus for you" (1 Thessalonians 5:18).

For many Christians this is exactly where the battle is won or lost. After examining themselves, confessing all known sin, yielding themselves to God, and asking for His filling, they are faced with a decision—to believe they are filled or to go away in unbelief, in which case they have sinned, for "whatever is not from faith is sin" (Romans 14:23).

Sometimes the same Christians who tell new converts that they should "take God at His word" concerning salvation find it difficult to heed their own advice concerning the filling of the Holy Spirit. Oh, that we might believe God when He says, "How much more will your heavenly Father give the Holy Spirit to those who ask Him!" (Luke 11:13).

If you have fulfilled the first four steps to being filled with the Spirit, then thank God for His filling by faith. Don't wait for feelings, don't wait for any physical signs, but fasten your faith to the Word of God and believe that He will fill you with His Spirit.

Feelings of assurance of the Spirit's filling often follow our taking God at His word and believing He has filled us. But these neither cause the filling nor determine whether or not we are filled. Believing we are filled with the Spirit is merely taking God by faith at His word.

WALKING IN THE SPIRIT

"I say then: Walk in the Spirit, and you shall not fulfill the lust of the flesh" (Galatians 5:16).

"If we live in the Spirit, let us also walk in the Spirit" (Galatians 5:25).

"Walking in the Spirit" and being filled by the Holy Spirit are not one and the same thing, though they are very closely related. Having followed the five simple rules for the filling of the Holy Spirit, we can walk in the Spirit by guarding against quenching or grieving the Spirit. This means we must repeat the above five steps each time we become aware that sin has crept into our lives.

Though we can be filled with the Holy Spirit in a moment of time, being filled with the Holy Spirit is not a single experience that lasts for life. On the contrary, it must be repeated many times. In fact, at first it should be done while kneeling at your place of devotion, at the breakfast table, in the car en route to work, while sweeping the kitchen floor, listening to a telephone conversation—anywhere. In effect, walking in the Spirit puts one in continual communion with God, which is the same as abiding in Christ. And walking in the Spirit requires daily feeding on the Word.

To "walk in the Spirit" is to be freed of your weaknesses. Yes, even your greatest weaknesses can be overcome by the Holy Spirit. Instead of being dominated by your weaknesses, you can be dominated by the Holy Spirit. That is God's will for all believers! When His Spirit fills our hearts and controls our lives, we will live differently—and everyone will notice the difference. We will not be full of ourselves. We will be full of Him. People will see Jesus Christ on display in our lives and be drawn to Him.

Only then will our hearts be saturated in His Spirit.

II

Living
in the Spirit

The fruit of the Spirit is love, joy, peace, longsuffering, gentleness, goodness, faith, meekness, temperance . . .
—GALATIANS 5:22–23 KJV

THE KEY TO A POSITIVE AND DYNAMIC LIFE IS THE transforming power of God's Spirit. The Spirit-filled personality does not have weaknesses. It has the strengths of the Holy Spirit. This is God's resource for the human weaknesses that result from our fallen human nature.

Anyone filled with the Holy Spirit is going to manifest these nine spiritual characteristics—called "the fruit of the Spirit" in Galatians 5:22. Spirit-filled Christians will have their own natural strengths, maintaining their individuality, but they will not be dominated by their natural weaknesses. The nine characteristics of the Spirit can transform those weaknesses into strengths.

All of these characteristics—love, joy, peace, long-suffering, gentleness, goodness, faith, meekness, and temperance or self-control—are illustrated in the life of Jesus Christ, the supreme example of the Spirit-controlled man. He, of course, had no weaknesses—only strengths—being God in human flesh. A fascinating study of the life of Christ would be to catalog these nine characteristics as they appear in the life of Christ.

These characteristics represent what God wants each of His children to be. They are not the result of our own human effort, but the supernatural result of the Holy Spirit controlling every area of our lives. Needless to say, anyone manifesting these characteristics is going to be a happy, well-adjusted, mature, and very fruitful human being. Every child of God longs to live this kind of life. But we can miss what God has for us if we allow our hearts to be filled with everything the world has to offer and little of what God has for us.

LOVE

The first characteristic in God's catalog of Spirit-filled traits is love—love for God and for our fellowmen. The Lord Jesus said, "You shall love the Lord your God with all your heart, with all your soul, and with all your mind" (Matthew 22:37), and He also said, "You shall love your neighbor as yourself" (Matthew 19:19).

Very honestly, this kind of love is supernatural! We are greedy and selfish creatures by nature. A love that causes someone to be more interested in the kingdom of God than in this earthly material kingdom is supernatural.

As for love of neighbor—there are some people with strong humanitarian tendencies by nature who have expressed love in exemplary acts. But the love described here is not just for those who stir admiration or compassion in us. The Lord Jesus said, "Love your enemies, bless those who curse you, do good to those who hate you, and pray for those who spitefully use you" (Matthew 5:44). This kind of love is never generated humanly but can only be effected by God. In fact, one of the thrilling evidences of the supernatural in the Christian experience is to see two people who have "personality conflicts" grow to genuinely love and appreciate each other.

Jesus tells us, "By this all will know that you are My disciples, if you have love for one another" (John 13:35). Many a church heartache could have been avoided had the filling of the Holy Spirit been sought for this first fruit of the Spirit.

This supernatural love is not limited by temperament or personality. If the Spirit controls a person's life—any person's life—that individual will be compassionate, tenderhearted, and loving. He or she will display the evidence of God's love in his or her heart by learning to love others as well.

If you would like to test your love for God, try this simple method given by the Lord Jesus. He said, "If you love Me, keep My commandments" (John 14:15). Just ask yourself, *Am I obedient to His commandments as revealed in His Word?* If not, you are not filled with the Holy Spirit. Loving God with all your heart will change your life and be used of God to change others as well.

JOY

The second temperament characteristic of the Spirit-filled person is joy. In his commentary on Galatians, R. C. H. Lenski, a great Lutheran theologian, gave this comment concerning the gracious emotion of joy:

> Yes, joy is one of the cardinal Christian virtues; it deserves a place next to love. Pessimism is a grave fault. This is not fatuous joy such as the world accepts; it is the enduring joy that bubbles up from all the grace of God in our possession, from the blessedness that is ours, that is undimmed by tribulation.[1]

The joy provided by the Holy Spirit is not limited by circumstances. Many have the mistaken idea that they can be happy if their circumstances work out properly. But they have confused happiness with joy. John Hunter of Capernwray, England, says, "Happiness is something that just happens because of the arrangement of circumstances, but joy endures in spite of circumstances."

The joy of the Spirit-filled life is characterized by looking not at circumstances but by "looking unto Jesus, the author and finisher of our faith" (Hebrews 12:2). As we look to Him, we see that "all things work together for good to those who love God, to those who are the called according to His purpose" (Romans 8:28).

In the Scripture "joy" and "rejoicing" are frequently presented as expected forms of Christian behavior. They are not the result of self-effort, but are the work of the Holy Spirit. As you look to Christ, the Spirit allows you to "commit your way to the LORD, trust also in Him, and He shall bring it to pass" (Psalm 37:5). The psalmist's prayer refers to the spiritual person's experience: "You [Lord] have put gladness in my heart, more than in the season that their grain and wine increased" (Psalm 4:7).

The apostle Paul, writing from a prison dungeon, said, "Rejoice in the Lord always. Again I will say, rejoice!" (Philippians 4:4). How could he say that? Because he had learned to experience the Spirit-filled life. And from the same prison cell he said, "I have learned in whatever state I am, to be content" (Philippians 4:11). Anyone who can rejoice and be content while in prison has to have a super-natural source of power!

The Philippian jailer saw the genuine and supernatural joy reflected in the lives of Paul and Silas when thrown into jail for preaching the gospel. He heard their singing and praising the Lord and must have been deeply impressed.

This joy of the Spirit is woefully lacking in many Christians today, and that lack keeps them from being fruitful in winning people to Christ. To be attracted to Christ, the world must see some evidence of what He can do in the life of the believer.

This supernatural joy is available for any Christian regardless of his or her experiences. Jesus said, "These things I have spoken to you, that My joy may remain in you, and that your joy may be full" (John 15:11). He also stated in John 10:10, "I have come that they may have life, and that they may have it more abundantly." That abundant life will reveal itself in the Christian through joy, even under adverse circumstances, but it is only possible as the Christian is filled with the Holy Spirit.

Martin Luther said:

God does not like doubt and dejection. He hates dreary doctrine, gloom and melancholy thought. God likes cheerful hearts. He did not send His son to fill us with sadness, but to gladden our hearts. Christ says: "Rejoice for your names are written in heaven."[2]

PEACE

The third temperament trait of the Spirit-filled life is peace. Since the Bible should always be interpreted in the light of its context, let's examine the context of the list of the fruit of the Spirit—the verses in Galatians 5 just preceding these nine characteristics. There Paul describes not only the works of the natural man without the Spirit, but also the natural emotions: hatred, contentions, jealousies, outbursts of wrath, selfish ambitions, dissensions, heresies, and envy (verses 20–21). We see that the farther we go from God, the less we know of peace.

The peace that is a characteristic of the Spirit-filled life is really twofold. Someone has described it as "peace with God" and the "peace of God." The Lord Jesus said, "Peace I leave with you, My peace I give to you" (John 14:27). The peace He "leaves with" us might be called "peace with God." This peace with God is the result of salvation by faith. Human beings outside of Jesus Christ know nothing of peace in relationship with God because their sin is ever before them. They know they are accountable before God at the judgment. This nagging fear robs a person of peace with God.

But when this individual takes Jesus Christ at His word and invites Him into his or her life as Lord and Savior, Jesus Christ not only comes in as He promised (see Revelation 3:20), but He also immediately cleanses all that person's sin (see 1 John 1:7, 9). When the realization of God's forgiveness really grips a heart, that person has peace with God. As Romans 5:1 says, "Therefore, having been justified by faith, we have peace with God through our Lord Jesus Christ."

The Spirit-filled Christian has a second peace: the peace Christ gives us, or "the peace of God"—the peace of an untroubled heart. Jesus said, "My peace I give to you; not as the world gives do I give to you. Let not your heart be troubled, neither let it be afraid"(John 14:27). The preceding verse describes the Holy Spirit as "the Comforter (KJV)." So here our Lord said that the Holy Spirit would be the source of the "peace of God."

The peace *of* God, which is the antidote to worry, is not so automatically possessed by Christians as the peace *with* God. The peace *of* God—peace untroubled in the face of difficult circumstances—is illustrated by the Lord Jesus, who was sound asleep in the lower part of the ship, while the twelve disciples were frightened beyond rationality (see Matthew 8:23–27).

That ratio of twelve to one is similar to that evident among Christians today. It seems that when life's seas become turbulent, twelve Christians will fret and fume and worry, while only one will have enough inner peace to trust God to take care of the circumstances. The twelve will be prone to worry all night, which further complicates their emotional, physical, and spiritual lives, while the one who "believes God" will get a good night's sleep, awaken re-freshed, and be available for God's use the next day.

Circumstances—subject to change—should never be the basis of our peace. Even becoming a Christian does not spare us from difficult circumstances. Real, consistent peace is found as we look to God and allow the Holy Spirit to supply us with one of life's greatest treasures: "the peace of God." The apostle Paul described this peace this way: "Be anxious for nothing, but in everything by prayer and supplication, with thanks-giving, let your requests be made known to God; and the peace of God, which surpasses all understanding, will guard your hearts and minds through Christ Jesus" (Philippians 4:6–7). An untroubled, unworried individual facing the cir-cumstances of life possesses a peace "which surpasses all under-standing." That is the "peace of God" that the Holy Spirit longs to give to every believing heart.

These first three characteristics, love, joy, and peace, are emotions that counteract the most common weaknesses of our lives, including cruelty, anger, indifference, pessimism, gloom, and criticism. They stand as adequate reasons for living the Spirit-filled life, but this is only the beginning.

LONG-SUFFERING

The fourth trait of the Spirit-filled person is long-suffering—or patience and endurance. A very simple definition of *long-*

suffering is "to suffer long." Long-suffering involves the ability to bear injuries or suffer reproof or affliction without answering in kind. Consider what the apostle Peter said about the Lord Jesus: "When He was reviled, [He] did not revile in return; when He suffered, He did not threaten" (1 Peter 2:23). That's long-suffering. Jesus stood up under the pressure.

A long-suffering person is one who can do the menial, forgotten, and difficult tasks of life without complaining or seething, but graciously, as unto the Lord. This person finishes a task or suffers affronts while manifesting the loving Spirit of Christ. An old-time preacher once said, "The greatest ability is dependability."

GENTLENESS

The fifth characteristic of the Spirit-filled life is what the King James Version calls "gentleness." Most of the modern translators of the Greek New Testament render this as "kindness" or "goodness." These alternate translations of the word lessen the importance of the tender-heartedness that motivates thoughtful, polite, gracious, considerate acts of kindness. The world in which we live knows little of such tender-heartedness. It is the result of the compassion of the Holy Spirit for a lost and dying humanity.

The hurrying, bustling, and pressurized life we live today tends to make even some of the finest of Christians annoyed at the interruptions of "the little people." Jesus' gentle spirit can be contrasted with the disciples' cruel attitude toward the children who had been brought to Jesus for a blessing. While the disciples rebuked those who brought them, Jesus said, "Let the little children come to Me, and do not forbid them" (Mark 10:13).

This gentle characteristic of the Holy Spirit never asks, "How often must I forgive my brother when he sins against me?" or, "Should I forgive a brother who does not ask for forgiveness?" or, "Isn't there a limit to how much a person can stand?" The Holy Spirit is able to produce gentleness in the face of all the pressures and problems of life.

Jesus, who possessed the Holy Spirit without measure, pictured Himself as a shepherd gently caring for His vulnerable sheep (John 10:11–18). Today, He continues that care through the ministry of His Spirit in the lives of His people. We are the instruments of His care, kindness, and gentleness.

GOODNESS

The sixth characteristic of the Spirit-filled life is goodness, which is defined as one who is "generous of self and possessions." It is benevolence in its purest sense. It includes hospitality and all acts of goodness that flow from the unselfish heart that is more interested in giving than receiving. Paul told Titus, the young preacher, that he should preach so "those who have believed in God should be careful to maintain good works" (Titus 3:8).

We postmoderns are so selfish by nature that we need to be reminded by the Word of God and the indwelling Holy Spirit to focus our efforts on goodness. This characteristic then describes a person who is more interested in doing for others than for himself.

People, by nature, are prone to be inconsiderate and selfish. All of us need this trait of goodness. It is particularly needed by those with tendencies toward depression and gloom, caused by an overindulgence in self-centered thought patterns. There is something therapeutic about doing for others that lifts a person out of the rut of self-thought. As the Lord Jesus said, "It is more blessed to give than to receive" (Acts 20:35).

Many Christians have cheated themselves out of a blessing by not obeying the Holy Spirit's inspired impulse to do something good or kind for someone else. Instead of bringing joy to someone else's life by that act of kindness, the self-centered person stifles the impulse and sinks deeper and deeper in the slough of despondency and gloom. It is one thing to get good impulses; it is quite another to transmit them into acts of goodness. D. L. Moody once stated that it was his custom, after presenting himself to the Holy Spirit and asking to be led by the Spirit, to act upon the impulses that came to his mind, provided they did not violate any known truth of Scripture.[3] Generally speaking, that is a good rule to follow, for it pays rich dividends in mental health in the life of the giver.

FAITH

The seventh trait of the Spirit-filled life is faith. It involves a complete abandonment to God and an absolute dependence upon Him. It is a perfect antidote to fear, which causes worry, anxiety, and panic.

Some commentators suggest that "faith" in Galatians 5:22 involves more than faith in God; it involves faithfulness or dependability. But actually, a person who has Spirit-inspired faith in God will be faithful and dependable. When the Spirit is in control, life goes forward under the full conviction of God's ability and power.

In a vital way faith is the key to many other Christian graces. If we really believe God is able to supply all our needs, our faith will nurture peace and joy and crowd out doubt, fear, striving, and many other works of the flesh. Many of God's people, like the nation of Israel, waste "forty years" out in the desert of life because they do not believe God. Far too many Christians have "grasshopper vision." They are like the ten faithless spies sent to scout out the Promised Land. They saw giants there and came back to report, "We were like grasshoppers . . . in their sight" (Numbers 13:33). How could they possibly know what the giants thought of them? You can be sure they did not get close enough to ask! They did just what we often do—jumped to a faithless conclusion. Unbelief, which causes fear, always limits God's use of our lives.

The Bible teaches that there are two sources of faith. The first is the Word of God in the life of the believer. Romans 10:17 states, "Faith comes by hearing, and hearing by the word of God." The second is the Holy Spirit, as made clear here in Galatians 5:22. If your heart is open to doubts, indecision, and fear, then as a believer you can look to the filling of the Holy Spirit to give you a heart of faith that will dispel these emotions and their self-limiting actions. It may not happen overnight; habits are binding chains, but God gives the victory in Christ Jesus. "Wait on the LORD; be of good courage, and He shall strengthen your heart; wait, I say, on the LORD!" (Psalm 27:14).

MEEKNESS

The eighth temperament trait of the Holy Spirit's filling is meekness. The natural person is proud, haughty, arrogant, egotistical, and self-centered, but when the Holy Spirit fills a heart, that person will become humble, mild, submissive, and easily entreated.

Jesus is the greatest example of meekness. The Creator of humankind was beaten, ridiculed, abused, and spat upon by His own creation. The Creator of the universe was willing to humble Himself, take on the form of a servant, and become subject to the whims of humanity, even to the point of death, that He might purchase our redemption by his blood. He said of Himself, "I am meek and lowly in heart" (Matthew 11:29 KJV).

His meek spirit is especially evident in the hours of His suffering. Consider the resources at His disposal: "Do you think that I cannot now pray to My Father, and He will provide Me with more than twelve legions of angels? How then could the Scriptures be fulfilled, that it must happen thus?" (Matthew 26:53–54).

Such meekness is not natural! Only the supernatural indwelling Spirit of God could cause any of us to react to physical or emotional persecution in meekness. It is a natural tendency to assert one's self, but even the most angry temperament can be controlled by the filling of the Holy Spirit and made to manifest this admirable trait of meekness.

SELF-CONTROL

The final characteristic of the Spirit-filled believer is self-control. The King James Version uses the word *temperance,* which means self-control or self-discipline.

Our natural inclination is to follow the path of least resistance. The sanguines probably have more temptation along this line than any of the other temperament types, though who hasn't given in to this very common temptation? Self-control will solve the Christian's problem of emotional outbursts, such as rage, anger, fear, and jealousy, and rein in emotional excesses of any kind. The Spirit-controlled temperament will be consistent, dependable, and well-ordered.

The one challenge all believers face is an inconsistent or ineffective devotional life. No Christian can be mature in Christ, steadily filled with the Holy Spirit, and fully used by God who does not regularly feed on the Word of God. Knowing the truth is vital to doing the truth.

As you look at these nine admirable traits of the Spirit-filled person, you get a picture not only of what God wants you to be, but also of what He is willing to make you in spite of your natural tendencies. But remember, no amount of self-improvement or self-effort can bring any of these traits into our lives without the power of the Holy Spirit. From this we conclude that the single most important thing in the life of any Christian is to be filled with the Holy Spirit—only under His influence can we hope to become all that God wants us to be.

12

Saturated
with Truth

And you shall know the truth,
and the truth shall make you free.
—JOHN 8:32

A MIND DEVOID OF TRUTH PRODUCES A HEART without hope. The emptiness of our times is a reflection of the emptiness of our hearts. We cannot satisfy the restlessness of our hearts without the anchor of truth in the Word of God. Only by filling our minds with God's truth can we hope to offset the heart failure of our secular cultures, let alone our personal lives.

Here is what Bible reading and personal study will do for you:

1. It Will Make You a Strong Christian

No one wants to be a weakling, whether physically or spiritually. The "young men" of 1 John 2:14 were no longer "children" but were "strong" because the Word of God lived in them and they overcame the wicked one. This means they had fed on the Word of God until they had grown strong enough in the faith that they were not continually defeated by sin and temptation. There is only one possible way to grow strong spiritually—by reading and studying the Word of God.

Christians may vary in their intelligence—some brilliant, some average, some with college backgrounds; some are scarcely educated, and some go to Bible college, but most do not. From each of these groups, some Christians remain continual babies while others grow strong in the Lord. The thing they have in common is not their mutual gifts of education but *whether or not they develop the habit of daily feeding their minds on the Word of God.*

Note the expression in 1 John 2:14: "You have overcome the wicked one." This takes spiritual strength that comes only from a study of the Word of God. Of the hundreds of spiritual failures, the thing they all have in common is an absence of the Word in their daily lives. All these failures (and consequent miseries) could have been avoided if these people had learned to study the Word for themselves.

2. It Will Assure You of Your Salvation

The first thing every young Christian needs is to be absolutely certain he is a Christian. Salvation is so marvelous—a free gift from a loving God—that it seems too good to be true. Consequently one of the first difficulties a new convert runs into after he has left the one who led him to Christ is entertaining doubts about his salvation. The *only source* of assurance is the Bible! But what good is this to him if he doesn't read the Bible for himself?

The promises and guarantees of God are of little value hidden between the covers of a Bible; Christians need them on the frontal lobes of their brain. And that is the reason the Bible was written. Listen to 1 John again, chapter 5, verse 13: "These things I have written to you who believe in the name of the Son of God, *that you may know that you have eternal life*" (emphasis added).

The Christian who has an abiding assurance that he is a child of God and that God is *his* heavenly Father has the basis for a sound emotional life. The vast majority of Christians with fears, worries, and other emotional foibles lack assurance of salvation because they have been heeding their minds instead of reading their Bibles.

No one will be assured of God when he is limited to the thoughts of his mind, because as the Bible teaches, the concept of God does not come by thinking, but by the "wisdom of God" in the Scriptures (1 Corinthians 1:21). If you want to enjoy the assurance of your salvation, then begin to study the Word of God regularly, for this is the only place you will find it.

3. It Will Give You Confidence and Power in Prayer

Now that you are a Christian you can talk to your heavenly Father about anything you have on your heart. But how do you know He is listening? Because He says so in His Word—in many places. 1 John 5:14–15 teaches that we can pray in confidence that He hears us. In John 15:7 our Lord promised, "If ye abide in me, and my words abide in you, ye shall ask what ye will, and it shall be done unto you" (KJV). This means that Bible study (which is how His words abide in us) gives us power in prayer, because as we study God's Word we become acquainted with His will and consequently learn how to pray.

Confucius was once asked by one of his students, "Does it help to pray for our sins?" to which he is said to have replied, "I'm not sure, but it can't hurt to try." That is no help at all! Only the Bible teaches that God does in fact answer prayer, and only the Bible-taught Christian fully enjoys that confidence.

4. It Will Cleanse You from Sin

Lady Macbeth was not the first to cry out in anguish of soul because of the guilt-consciousness of her sin. Guilt is a universal problem, and billions of people have no idea where to go for cleansing. But guilt should never bother a Bible-taught Christian because our Lord said, "Now ye are clean through the word which I have spoken unto you" (John 15:3 KJV). The Word of God has a cleansing effect upon the believer. Our Lord prayed, "Sanctify them through thy truth; thy word is truth" (John 17:17). The Word of God has a powerful cleansing effect on the Christian who studies it.

A father was once asked by his son to explain how the Word of God cleansed a person. Instead of answering, he asked his son to take a wicker basket down to the lake and bring him a basketful of water. The lad tried several times, but before he got back to where his dad was, the basket was empty. In frustration, he complained to his father, "It's impossible—before I get it here, the water has all run out!" The father then called the boy's attention to how clean the basket was, and said, "That is how the Word of God cleanses the believer as it passes through his mind."

How do we know that our sins are forgiven? Because the Bible says, "If we confess our sins, he is faithful and just to forgive us our sins, and to cleanse us from all unrighteousness" (1 John 1:9 KJV). What encouragement it gives us to know that God is faithful in the work of cleansing!

As a Christian, you need to know what is sin and what is not. God has not left you to your own judgment. He says, "Wherewithal shall a young man cleanse his way? By taking heed thereto according to thy word" (Psalm 119:9 KJV). Studying the Bible will cleanse you from sin and warn you of sin.

When I was a young Christian, I (Tim) asked a visiting minister to sign my Bible, which he did, but he also added a note that is very perceptive: "This book will keep you from sin or sin will keep you from this book."

5. It Will Give You Joy

One of the blessings of the Christian life is joy, but often that joy is stifled by the problems of life. Our Lord said, "These things have I spoken unto you, that my joy might remain in you, and that your joy might be full"(John 15:11 KJV). If you read the writings of mankind or look at the problems that surround you, your joy will turn to fear, dread, or sometimes depression.

During a financial recession, I attended a meeting of the church board of trustees. As I listened to the men talk, it sounded as though the Lord had gone out of business—all they did was forecast gloom, doom, and despair. Finally I asked, "What have you men been reading lately?" They replied, *"The Wall Street Journal, U.S. News and World Report,*

The San Diego Union," etc. So I replied, "You've been read-ing the wrong material!" It is the *Word of God* that puts joy in our hearts regardless of the circumstances.

6. It Will Produce Peace in Your Life

One of the supernatural evidences of the Christian life is peace in one's heart when the circumstances of life call for worry and anxiety. Now that you have received Christ as your Savior and Lord, you have a right to expect to be different, and your friends are justified in expecting to see that difference. When a supernatural power like the Holy Spirit comes to live in your life, you will be dif-ferent. That difference is primarily shown in your emo-tions, which will be characterized by peace in the face of difficulties. But if the Word of God does not "dwell in you richly" by reading and study, it will not produce the peace that should characterize your life.

Jesus Christ said, "These things have I spoken unto you that in me ye might have peace. In the world ye shall have tribulation; but be of good cheer, I have overcome the world" (John 16:33). What makes this statement of particu-lar interest is that our Lord gave this message to His disciples just before the turmoil that resulted in His crucifixion. As His disciples faced this impending crisis, He wanted them to have *peace* through His Word.

For almost two thousand years God's people have

fortified themselves for the crises of life by reading and studying the Bible. That's what God meant when He said, "Let the peace of God rule in your hearts, to the which also ye are called in one body, and be ye thankful" (Colossians 3:15 KJV). Peace is not automatic. We let it flood our hearts through filling our minds with the promises, principles, and faithfulness of God as taught in His Word. Many a Christian businessman who reads the *Wall Street Journal* or *Time* magazine daily instead of his Bible becomes upset at monetary conditions, when all the time God wants to flood his heart with peace through the daily reading of His Word.

7. It Will Guide You in Making Important Decisions of Life

Life is filled with decisions—little ones, big ones, and many in between. When the principles of God are well known to a Christian, this simplifies the process of decision making. That's what Scripture means when it says, "Thy word is a lamp unto my feet, and a light unto my path" (Psalm 119:105 KJV). The principles of God serve as a guide in reaching decisions.

Today's "situational ethics" philosophy is a chaotic approach to life that produces much harm. It is far better to program biblical principles into your mind in advance of a crisis than to wait until emotions, passions, and life pressures close in on you and then try to decide what to do. As the Lord Himself said, "Blessed [happy] are those who hear the word of God and keep it" (Luke 11:28). You cannot keep what you have not heard! But as you fill your mind daily with the Word of God, it will enlighten the dark paths of the future with divine guidance.

8. It Will Enable You to Articulate Your Faith

Most of the people you meet in life are ignorant of biblical concepts. Many of these have questions or doubts and need someone who knows the Bible to guide them. God challenges us, "Sanctify the Lord God in your hearts, and always be ready to give a defense to everyone who asks you a reason for the hope that is in you, with meekness and fear" (1 Peter 3:15). The only way you will be able to answer the questioner, scorner, or sincere seeker of truth is to be ready always to answer them by daily reading and studying the Word.

A Navy lieutenant who claimed to have been a Christian for eleven years said, "I never have an opportunity to share my faith with anyone." It seemed incredible to me that a man stationed aboard an aircraft carrier with three thousand other men couldn't find someone to share Christ with, but I ignored his comment and started him on a Bible reading, studying, and learning program.

Two months later, when he came in for his weekly checkup, he told me about leading his first soul to Christ. Then he reminded me of his previous comment and said,

"My problem wasn't lack of opportunity; I just didn't know what to do when one came along. Now my mind is so filled with the Word of God that I'm sharing it all the time. Before I started studying the Bible I just didn't know what to say." That young man's experience could be multiplied many times, for you cannot communicate what you do not know. Almost every Christian wants to be fruitful and to effectively share Christ with others, but this is totally impossible without at least an elementary knowledge of the Word of God.

9. It Will Guarantee Your Success!

Everyone wants to be successful. This doesn't mean riches or fame; you can have those without having true success. Rather, we yearn to succeed. That's why how-to or success-oriented books are so popular today. No one reads books on how to fail!

Joshua 1:8 tells us, "This Book of the Law shall not depart from your mouth, but you shall meditate in it day and night, that you may observe to do according to all that is written in it. For then you will make your way prosperous, and then you will have good success." Note the words "and then you will have good success." Daily meditation (thinking) on the Word of God produces the success that everyone desires. Certainly it did for Joshua. Many Christian businessmen have claimed this same promise, and today testify to God's faithfulness.

Lest you think that God's promise to Joshua was an isolated one, we should look at the formula for happiness found in the first psalm: "Blessed is the man that walketh not in the counsel of the ungodly, nor standeth in the way of sinners, nor sitteth in the seat of the scornful. But his delight is in the law of the LORD, and in his law doth he meditate day and night. And he shall be like a tree planted by the rivers of water, that bringeth forth his fruit in its season; his leaf also shall not wither, and whatsoever he doeth shall prosper" (Psalm 1:1–3 KJV). That kind of daily productivity comes from daily feeding one's mind on the Word of God.

Unfortunately, many Christians think they are too busy to refresh their minds each day on the Word of God. What they don't realize is that a daily quiet time costs them nothing in the long run because the rest of their day will be more successful than if they had ignored their Bibles. A brilliant neurosurgeon in Atlanta claims, "The most important part of my day is the first thirty minutes after awaking, so I spend twenty minutes of it reading and studying the Word of God. It enriches the rest of my day." Try it—you'll like it!

10. It Will Satisfy Your Heart

The Bible emphasizes the spiritual connection between the mind and the heart. Psalm 119:2 says, "Blessed are they that keep his testimonies (words), and that seek him with the whole heart." Psalm 119 is the longest chapter in the whole

Bible. It contains 176 verses and every one of them mentions the word of God (ways, testimonies, precepts, laws, statutes, decrees, commands, etc.). In verse 11, the psalmist declares: "Your word I have hidden in my heart that I might not sin against You." In verse 24, he states: "Your statues also are my delight and my counselors." In verse 28, he cries: "My soul is weary with sorrows; strengthen me according to your word" (NIV). In verse 30, he adds: "I have chosen the way of truth; I have set my heart on your laws" (NIV).

Nothing can satisfy the longing of the human heart like God's truth. It cuts through all the deceptions of life and tells us what we need to hear. Have you ever had an experience when someone was in the middle of lying to you and suddenly broke down and told the truth? All of a sudden, everything made sense in light of the truth.

That is how God's Word is to the human heart. As you read it, God speaks to you, and something inside of you says, *Yes—this is true.*

Jesus said, "You shall know the truth, and the truth shall make you free" (John 8:32). God's truth has liberating power for the human heart. It can unlock its secrets, reveal its hidden sins, and transform its darkness into light. Let it saturate your mind and it will change your heart—forever.

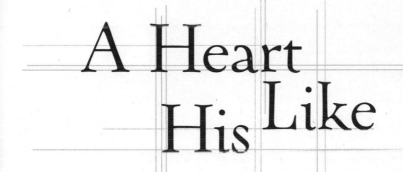

A Heart
His Like

13

Finding
God's Heart

Blessed are the pure in heart,
for they shall see God.
—MATTHEW 5:8

THE SUN WAS COMING UP OVER THE OCEAN AS
Shannon and Kari walked along the beach. The morning
sand was still undisturbed as they took their early morning
stroll.

"There's something about the solitude of early morning
that really makes me think." Shannon glanced at her sister
and kept walking.

"About what?" Kari slowed her steps, staring out at the still
dark sea. She had been sharing the truth of Christ with her sister and wondered if finally her sister had chosen to listen.

"About everything. About life. About God," Shannon replied.

"Really?" A ripple of joy made its way across Kari's heart.

Shannon stopped walking and drew a deep breath. "You're right, Sis. I've been running away from God. I've tried everything else, and my heart just isn't satisfied."

"I've been there." Kari started walking again, and Shannon fell in beside her.

"It's like something's missing every minute of the day." Shannon's hair blew in the wind. "I guess it's taken me all this time to admit it to myself."

"Exactly." A sea gull's cry punctuated their conversation. Kari watched it soar across the water. "I got tired of the guys, the parties, the alcohol, the drugs. One morning, I woke up and looked at my whole miserable life and realized it wasn't worth it!"

"So you turned to God, right?"

"Not at first." Kari shrugged. "I still had a lot of questions, but never any answers. Eventually the emptiness in my heart drove me to God."

"It's taken me longer." Shannon stopped and faced her sister. There were tears in her eyes when she spoke again. "But I'm ready now. I want to know God like you do. I want my heart to be at peace like yours is."

They came together in an embrace that reached back into their childhood. It was a deep, soul-cleansing hug that reminded them of the bond they would always share. Tears and smiles followed. Then, they took each other's hands and prayed together as the morning sun glistened off their faces.

In those quiet moments, Shannon gave her heart to Christ. It was the beginning of a brand-new life. Her heart felt changed. And so did everything else.

The Bible tells us: "Let us draw near to God with a sincere heart in full assurance of faith, having our hearts sprinkled to cleanse us from a guilty conscience and having our bodies washed with pure water" (Hebrews 10:22). The only real hope for the human condition is a heart-transforming experience with God. We cannot change ourselves, because our hearts are "deceitful above all things and beyond cure" (Jeremiah 17:9 NIV). God alone can give us a "new heart" and put within us a "new spirit" (Ezekiel 36:26).

SPIRITUAL TRANSFORMATION

Finding the heart of God involves admitting our own spiritual inadequacy. It means coming to the end of ourselves. Only when we finally realize that we can't change ourselves will we discover God's power to transform our hearts and change our lives. God alone is the ultimate Heart Surgeon. He alone can remove the heart of stone and replace it with a heart like His.

"I, the LORD, search the heart, I test the mind," God says (Jeremiah 17:10). His divine presence exposes our empty hearts and makes us realize our need for Him. "One of the hallmark claims of evangelical Christianity is this," writes Bruce Demarest, "we promise the new believer a heart connectedness to God through Christ. This promise comes right out of the gospel, which offers both a doctrine to believe and a restored relationship with the God of the universe to enjoy."[1]

Demarest challenges us to develop a heart for God, not just a belief in God. He reminds us that it is often easier to perform for God, rather than develop a relationship with God. We plod on in our repetitious spiritual routines— attending church, giving money, reading books, serving God. But often, we do not sense God really working in our lives. Or, we feel guilty because we think we are unworthy of His blessings.

Jesus challenged one of His own disciples when He asked, "Have I been with you so long, and yet you have not known Me?" (John 14:9). We will never be spiritually satisfied until we engage God's heart and let Him change our hearts. Demarest adds, "How astonishing that the infinite Creator of the universe should seek out undeserving people for heart-to-heart relationship. But that is what He does!"[2]

Finding the heart of God is a personal and spiritual journey. It is a relationship with Him, not just activity for

Him. It is personal intimacy, not mere intellectual pursuit. It is a spiritual communion with God, not just a metaphysical experience with God. Demarest is quick to remind us of the dangers of syrupy infatuation with God, rather than a heart-transforming experience with God. He writes, "You may know people who became infatuated with God in a sudden burst of energy that soon burned out. This kind of energy comes from being attracted to another for selfish reasons. It makes you feel good, but fails to genuinely engage the other person's soul . . . [or] inner being."[3]

Knowing God in the fullest sense means experiencing God in your heart. It begins by believing He wants to know you personally. Your first step of faith will ignite your soul with His presence. But it is only as you continue to be honest with Him and seek Him with all your heart that you will come to know Him intimately and deeply.

Romans 10:9–10 describes the initial step of faith like this: "That if you confess with your mouth, 'Jesus is Lord,' and believe in your heart that God has raised him from the dead, you will be saved. For it is with your heart that you believe and are justified, and it is with your mouth that you confess and are saved" (NIV). Believing that Jesus Christ died for our sins and rose from the dead is essential to our salvation. Jesus alone satisfies the demand of God for a righteous payment for our sins. It is not a question at this point whether our religion satisfies us. It only matters that it satisfied God. And God is only satisfied with the blood atonement of His Son on our behalf.

Leon Morris writes, "We know love in the New Testament sense only because we see it in the cross."[4] The cross of Christ shouts to us, "I love you! I did it all for you!" To see this love and to believe it is to be affected by it. As the hymn writer put it:

> When I survey the wondrous cross
> On which the Prince of Glory died,
> My richest gain I count but loss
> And pour contempt on all my pride.[5]

Once we have placed our faith in what Jesus did for us on the cross, our salvation is sealed forever. From this point on, what matters is our personal relationship with God. Now the question of our satisfaction is legitimate, because God will not allow us to be satisfied with anything less than a heart relationship with Him.

A HEART FOR GOD

When the prophet Samuel went searching for a new king for Israel, he announced. "The LORD does not look at the things man looks at. Man looks at the outward appearance, but the LORD looks at the heart" (1 Samuel 16:7 NIV). People have always been surprised at God's choices, because God does not see things as we do. He sees our hearts and judges our inner character. That is why the Bible so often uses the phrase "with all your heart" (Deuteronomy 4:29; 6:5; 10:12; 26:16; 30:6).

A survey of the biblical usage of the term "heart" reveals the following about our hearts.

Deceitful Heart

"The heart is deceitful above all things and beyond cure. Who can understand it?" (Jeremiah 17:9 NIV). The biblical picture of the unregenerate human heart is one of corruption and deceit. The sinfulness and selfishness of the heart leaves it incapable of spiritual satisfaction apart from the intervention of divine grace and spiritual regeneration. The natural deception of the human heart blinds us to the truth about God, ourselves, and others. It leaves us thinking that we don't need God's help. It tells us that we can make it on our own. And nothing could be further from the truth.

Sinful Heart

The root problem of the human heart is the fact that it is sinful. Psalm 66:18 says, "If I had cherished sin in my heart, the Lord would not have listened" (NIV). We cannot come to God in faith as long as we are holding on to our sin. Romans

3:23 tells us, "For all have sinned and fall short of the glory of God." It is because of our sin that we need a Savior. That is why John the Baptist said of Jesus, "Behold! The Lamb of God who takes away the sin of the world!" (John 1:29).

Guilty Heart

Job explains, "I have concealed my sin as men do, by hiding my guilt in my heart" (Job 31:33 NIV). There is something so humiliating about guilt that we would rather hide it than face it. But it is only in facing it that we ever really deal with it. This is why the Bible says, "If we confess our sins, He is faithful and just to forgive us our sins and to cleanse us from all unrighteousness" (1 John 1:9).

Proud Heart

The core of the unredeemed heart is pride. Proverbs 16:5 says: "The LORD detests all the proud of heart . . . They will not go unpunished" (NIV). Psalm 101:5 adds, "The one who has a haughty look and a proud heart, him will I not endure." God makes it very clear that pride keeps us from Him and it keeps Him from us. This is why it is necessary for our pride to be broken in order for our hearts to be changed by God.

Hard Heart

Whenever we persistently reject God, we are in danger of hardening our hearts against Him. God told Moses,

"Pharaoh's heart is unyielding" (Exodus 7:14 NIV). Another time, the Scripture says, "Pharaoh hardened his heart" (Exodus 8:32). In the New Testament, Jesus referred to hard hearts as the cause of marital conflicts and divorce (Matthew 19:8). This is why Jesus describes the hard heart in the Parable of the Sower as the hard ground that did not receive the "seed" of the gospel (Matthew 13:19).

Foolish Heart

The ultimate rejection of God comes when our hard hearts are foolish enough to suggest that God doesn't even exist. Psalms 14:1 and 53:1 state, "The fool has said in his heart, 'There is no God.'" Once we refuse to submit our hearts to God, we harden our hearts against God. When our hearts are fully hardened, we try to justify our unbelief by refusing to admit God exists. Romans 1:18–32 describes this process: "Their thinking became futile and their foolish hearts were darkened . . . Therefore God gave them over in the sinful desires of their hearts . . . they have become filled with every kind of wickedness" (NIV).

All we have to do is examine this biblical study of the heart and then analyze our culture accordingly. We should not be surprised by what we find. Our society reflects all the qualities of an unregenerate heart. Our culture is filled with pride, deceit, and guilt. Ours is a time of spiritual hardness, emptiness, and foolishness. We all know that we need help. But we can only find it when we turn our hearts toward God.

Broken Heart

People come to God when they come to the end of themselves. Only when we are truly broken will we turn to the One who can help us. The psalmist said, "The sacrifices of God are a broken spirit, a broken and a contrite heart—These, O God, You will not despise" (Psalm 51:17). The prophet Joel put it like this: "Return to me with all your heart, with fasting and weeping and mourning. Rend your heart and not your garments. Return to the LORD your God, for he is gracious and compassionate, slow to anger and abounding in love" (Joel 2:12–13 NIV).

Humble Heart

Once our hearts are broken before God, we are also humbled by God. Our pride is stripped away. Our excuses vanish. And our foolish rejection ceases. Instead of running away from God, we find ourselves running to God in humble submission to Him. Jesus said, "I tell you the truth, unless you change and become like little children, you will never enter the kingdom of heaven. Therefore, whoever humbles himself like this child is the greatest in the kingdom of heaven" (Matthew 18:3–4 NIV). Humility is the outward evidence of inward repentance. James said, "Humble yourselves before the Lord, and he will lift you up" (James 4:10 NIV).

Repentant Heart

Jesus warned, "But unless you repent, you will all likewise perish" (Luke 13:3). Repentance involves a change of mind and heart toward God and others. Jesus taught, "If your brother sins against you, rebuke him; and if he repents, forgive him" (Luke 17:3). Deuteronomy 4:29 says, "Seek the Lord your God—you will find him if you look for him with all your heart and with all your soul" (NIV). But the opposite is also true. Romans 2:5 warns, "Because of your stubbornness and your unrepentant heart, you are storing up wrath against yourself for the day of God's wrath, when his righteous judgment will be revealed" (NIV). This is why Jesus said, "There is rejoicing in the presence of the angels of God over one sinner who repents" (Luke 15:10).

Believing Heart

Romans 10:9 emphasizes, "That if you confess with your mouth the Lord Jesus and believe in your heart that God has raised Him from the dead, you will be saved." Romans 10:10 adds, "For with the heart one believes to righteousness." Hebrews 10:22 expresses the need for faith when it says, "Let us draw near to God with a true heart in full assurance of faith." The most basic promise in the New Testament says, "For God so loved the world that He gave His only begotten Son, that whoever believes in Him should not perish but have everlasting life" (John 3:16).

Transformed Heart

God promises to change our hearts if we will give them to Him. 2 Corinthians 5:17 promises, "Therefore, if anyone is in Christ, he is a new creation; the old has gone, the new has come!" (NIV). This is how Jesus could tell sinners, "Go now and leave your life of sin" (John 8:11 NIV). He was not asking them to change themselves. He was asking them to trust Him to be able to transform them. The psalmist put it like this: "Our fathers trusted in You; they trusted, and you delivered them. They cried to you, and were delivered; they trusted in You and were not ashamed" (Psalm 22:4–5).

Pure Heart

Purity of heart is the result of God's transforming grace in our lives. Jesus said, "Blessed are the pure in heart, for they shall see God" (Matthew 5:8). Romans 6:22 states: "But now that you have been set free from sin . . . the benefit you reap leads to holiness, and the result is eternal life" (NIV). Hebrews 12:14 warns, "Without holiness no one will see the Lord" (NIV). If we must be holy in order to see God, then how can sinful people ever hope for heaven? The answer is by having our hearts transformed by God and made pure and holy like His heart. The psalmist sang, "My flesh and my heart fail, but God is the strength of my heart and my portion forever" (Psalm 73:26). David, in repentance prayed, "Create in me a clean heart, O God, and renew a steadfast spirit within me" (Psalm 51:10).

Happy Heart

A changed heart is a happy heart. Psalm 13:5 declares, "But I trust in your unfailing love; my heart rejoices in your salvation" (NIV). Our hearts are happy because we are at peace with Him. Psalm 16:9 says, "Therefore my heart is glad, and my glory rejoices; my flesh also will rest in hope." When our hearts are right with God, we feel better physically and spiritually. Psalm 28:7 says, "My heart leaps for joy" (NIV). Proverbs 17:22 says, "A cheerful heart is good medicine" (NIV). Proverbs 15:13 adds, "A happy heart makes the face cheerful, but heartache crushes the spirit" (NIV). Nehemiah 8:10 adds, "The joy of the LORD is your strength." When your heart is right with God, it is filled with love, joy, and peace because God is in control.

KEEPING YOUR HEART

Once our hearts are transformed by God, we have a responsibility to maintain them. God is present in our lives through His indwelling Spirit. We are born again—from above by the regenerating power of the Holy Spirit (see John 3:1–16). Our lives are connected to God by the gift of eternal life. We will now live as long as God lives because He lives in us.

Too many Christians are willing to stop right here. They are on their way to heaven, and that's enough. Their focus is on the end of the journey, not the journey itself. Instead of enjoying the fullness of God's blessings in their lives, they short-circuit their own spiritual growth in a mundane and routine experience. Soon unconfessed sin corrodes our connection with God. Instead of speaking the truth from our hearts (see Psalm 15:2), we lie to ourselves, as well as God, about the condition of our hearts.

Soon our relationships with God suffer from a lack of honest communication with Him. We pull away from an intimate relationship with God because of guilt. We think that if we get too close to God, He will expose our sin—so we keep our distance. In some cases, we become so used to this distance that we "normalize" it. We choose our friends based on their levels of spirituality so we won't feel so guilty.

For others, it is simply a matter of getting so busy with the daily responsibilities of life that we stop spending time with God. We become like the person who skips his daily exercise for a few days thinking, "I can get back to this any-time." The next thing you know, weeks or months have gone by, and you have not taken time to get alone with God.

Theologian J. I. Packer observes: "The pace and pre-occupation of urbanized, mechanized, collectivized, secu-larized modern life are such that any sort of inner life is very hard to maintain . . . The concept of a Christian life as sanctified rush and bustle still dominates, and as a result, the experiential side of Christian holiness remains very much a closed book."[6]

Some Christians are uncomfortable talking about experiencing God in the life of the heart. Bruce Demarest reminds us, "A spirituality that embraces intellectual truth without personally engaging Christ in relationship is not Christian enough!"[7] Such a life becomes a dull routine of Christianized living on the lowest levels of personal piety and spirituality.

At the same time, Demarest warns, "Yet a life governed by emotion lacks theological controls and is in danger of drifting into doctrinal error and unfruitful practices."[8] He emphasizes the fact that the balanced Christian life involves three key elements: (1) reliable beliefs, (2) godly affections, (3) obedient action. All three are essential to effective Christian living. This is why we have to exercise spiritual discipline in keeping our hearts in tune with God.

Guarded Heart

Moses told the children of Israel to "take to heart" all the words God had spoken to them, so they could pass them on to their children (Deuteronomy 32:46 NIV). Joshua told them to serve the Lord "with all your heart and all your soul" (Joshua 22:5). The psalmist prayed, "Examine me, O LORD, and prove me; try my mind and my heart" (Psalm 26:2). In Psalm 139:23, he adds, "Search me, O God, and know my heart; try me, and know my anxieties." Proverbs 4:23 says, "Above all else, guard your heart, for it is the wellspring of life" (NIV). Proverbs 23:26 adds, "My son, give me your heart, and let your eyes observe my ways."

Steadfast Heart

We are told to guard our hearts against emotional temptations, so that our hearts will be fixed securely on God. Psalm 57:7 says, "My heart is steadfast, O God, my heart is steadfast; I will sing and give praise." The heart that is fixed on God is one that is free to worship God. Psalm 108:1 repeats the same idea. Psalm 112:7 adds, "He will have no fear of bad news; his heart is steadfast, trusting in the Lord" (NIV). Security and stability are the results of a fixed heart that is focused on God. Proverbs 3:5–6 summarizes this best when it says, "Trust in the LORD with all your heart, and lean not on your own understanding; in all your ways acknowledge Him, and He shall direct your paths."

Praying Heart

Prayers of the heart open the deepest core issues of our lives to the grace of God. They are the constant expressions of our hearts toward God. The apostle Paul referred to this when he told us to "pray without ceasing" (1 Thessalonians 5:17). The psalmist expresses this idea when he says, "My soul waits for the Lord more than those who watch for the morning" (Psalm 130:6). In Psalm 42:1–2, the psalmist cries, "As the deer pants for the water brooks, so pants my soul for You, O God. My soul thirsts for God, for the living God. When shall I come and appear before God?"

Hot Heart

We often hear people use the expression "keep your heart hot for God." This is actually a biblical expression. In 1 Thessalonians 5:19, Paul warned, "Do not put out the Spirit's fire" (NIV). In Ephesians 4:30, he wrote, "Do not grieve [KJV, "quench"] the Holy Spirit of God." Keeping our hearts hot is a result of keeping them right with God. The psalmist writes, "I trust in your unfailing love; my heart rejoices in your salvation" (Psalm 13:5 NIV). He adds, "My heart leaps for joy and I will give thanks to him in song" (Psalm 28:7 NIV). But Psalm 39:3 expresses it best: "My heart grew hot within me, and as I meditated, the fire burned" (NIV). His experience was like that of the prophet Jeremiah, to whom God said, "I will make My words in your mouth fire" (Jeremiah 5:14). The prophet himself said, "His word was in my heart like a burning fire" (Jeremiah 20:9). When our hearts are ablaze with the power and presence of God, others will see God at work in our lives.

Truth-Filled Heart

Jeremiah's heart was hot for God because it was filled with God's Word. The prophet said, "When your words came, I ate them; they were my joy and heart's delight" (Jeremiah 15:16 NIV). The psalmist also speaks of the importance of meditating and filling our hearts with God's Word. Psalm 19:14 says, "Let the words of my mouth and the meditation of my heart be acceptable in Your sight, O LORD, my strength and my redeemer."

Psalm 119, the longest chapter in the Bible, is filled with instructions about focusing our minds and hearts on God's truth. Verse 2 says, "Blessed are they who keep his statutes and seek him with all their heart" (NIV). Verse 10 adds, "I seek you with all my heart; do not let me go astray from your commands" (NIV). Verse 11 states, "Your word I have hidden in my heart, that I might not sin against You." Verse 30 adds, "I have chosen the way of truth; I have set my heart on your laws" (NIV). Verse 105 says, "Your word is a lamp to my feet and a light to my path." Verse 111 adds, "Your statutes are my heritage forever; they are the joy of my heart" (NIV).

Discerning Heart

When our hearts are saturated with God's Word, His truth gives us spiritual discernment. Proverbs 18:15 says, "The heart of the prudent acquires knowledge; and the ear of the wise seeks knowledge." Proverbs 21:2 adds, "Every way of a man is right in his own eyes, but the LORD weighs the hearts." Proverbs 23:12 challenges us to "apply your heart to instruction." Proverbs 22:17 tells us, "Incline your ear and hear the words of the wise, and apply your heart to my knowledge." Proverbs 23:15 promises, "My son, if your heart is wise, my heart will rejoice." When Solomon, the author of much of the Book of Proverbs, came to the throne of Israel, he prayed, "Give to your servant an understanding heart to judge Your people, that I may discern between good and evil" (1 Kings 3:9). As a result, 1 Kings 10:24 tells us, "The whole world sought audience with Solomon to hear the wisdom God had put in his heart" (NIV).

Godly Heart

The ultimate goal of the Christian life is to become like Christ. Romans 8:29 refers to this as being "conformed to the image of His Son." Jesus said of Himself, "Take My yoke upon you and learn from Me, for I am gentle and lowly in heart, and you will find rest for your souls" (Matthew 11:29). When our hearts are fixed on Christ, we will become like Him in every area of our lives. Paul said, "Your attitude should be the same as that of Christ Jesus" (Philippians 2:5 NIV). He urges us to be "like-minded, having the same love, being of one accord, of one mind" (Philippians 2:2). We may struggle to be like Him, but God promises to give us His grace to change our hearts and make them godly. The psalmist sings, "My flesh and my heart may fail, but God is the strength of my heart and my portion forever" (Psalm 73:26).

SPIRITUAL DISCIPLINE

Spiritual growth is a result of spiritual discipline. Just as physical exercise strengthens our physical bodies, so spiritual exercise enables us to be strengthened spiritually. Paul illustrated this in his letter to Timothy when he said, "Train yourself to be godly. For physical training is of some value, but godliness has value for all things, holding the promise for both the present life and the life to come" (1 Timothy 4:7–8 NIV). Bodily exercise profits a little bit and for a limited time, but spiritual discipline benefits both this life and our eternal relationship with God as well.

Ephesians 3:17 explains that God strengthens us with His power through His spirit in our inner being so "that Christ may dwell in your hearts through faith." At the point of our salvation, Christ comes to live within us. But it is throughout our sanctification (spiritual growth) that He takes control of the details of our lives. In the process, He continually makes us more and more like Himself. Our heart attitudes, our inner character, and our outward behavior are gradually transformed as our hearts reflect His heart, our attitudes reflect His attitudes, and our values reflect His values.

Salvation is a work of God's grace in our hearts. He draws us to Himself by the power of His love (displayed on the cross) and by the power of His Spirit (who convicts our hearts).[9] Sanctification is also a work of His grace, but it involves our cooperation as we are filled with His Spirit, as we pray, read His Word, study, contemplate, and meditate. That is why the Bible tells us to "Let the peace of God rule in your hearts," and to "Let the word of Christ dwell in you richly" (Colossians 3:15–16). These things do not happen automatically. They are a result of our practicing spiritual discipline in our lives.

Spirituality affects us *inwardly*, in that our hearts are being transformed by God's power. But spirituality also affects us *outwardly*, in that it transforms our relationships with others. We exhibit the "fruit of the Spirit" (Galatians 5:22–23) and the "gifts" of the Spirit (Romans 12:3–8). Our attitudes are conformed to the mind of Christ and are expressed by the actions of Christ (Philippians 2:5–11). We become servants to the needs of others. Our lives reflect the fact that Christ lives within us. Galatians 2:20 expresses it like this: "I have been crucified with Christ; it is no longer I who live, but Christ lives in me."

Jesus wants to make your heart (inner being) His home. He wants to live within your heart and life and make you like Himself. Humanly speaking, that seems like an impossibility. How can we be like Christ? By mystical contemplation? By disciplined imitation? By self-determination? No! Not at all. We can only be like Christ by turning our lives completely and totally over to Him. That is why Jesus came into our world in the first place. C. S. Lewis said, "The Son of God became man to enable men to become the sons of God."[10]

The choice is up to you. Will you open your heart to Him? If you will, you'll never be the same.

14

Forever His

Love the LORD your God with all your heart,
with all your soul, and with all your mind.
—MATTHEW 22:37

ROBERT STARED INTO HIS COFFEE CUP AND WONDERED why his friend was so happy. While Robert thought about the troubles in his marriage, Mark droned on about his newfound faith in God. Robert could hardly wait for their wives to finish shopping.

Anything to change the subject.

After thirty minutes, Robert no longer felt frustrated. Some of what Mark was saying actually sounded interesting. "You really believe this stuff?"

"Yes." Mark lightly punched Robert's shoulder. "Would I be telling you if I didn't?"

"What if . . ." Robert hesitated and stirred his coffee again. "What if I want to believe, too?"

Mark grinned. "Then you believe, buddy. It's that simple."

Robert shook his head. "Not really." His eyes narrowed. "Way back when I was a boy I raised my hand at an altar call. I remember waiting for something magical to happen that night, but it never did. Ever since then I've had a problem connecting my faith with my life. I mean, look at my marriage. Me and Kate are all but broken up."

"Tell me this." Mark's voice softened. "Are you happy?"

"Not really. In fact, not at all!"

"Then why not give God a try?"

Robert grimaced. "Because of the rules. I guess I'm still struggling with the whole issue of living the Christian life."

Mark smiled. "The rules everyone talks about are nothing more than safety rails on the path to happiness. Believe me, it's the only reason I'm loving life. I'm a changed man because of those so-called rules. And you can be, too."

Spirituality is a lifelong process. It is the realization that we were made to know God, and that we can't be fully satisfied until we do. There is a voice within the human soul that cries out for more than just a limited temporal existence. Augustine, the theologian, called it the "restless heart." Blaise Pascal, the philosopher, called it the God-shaped vacuum in the human soul. The apostle Paul said, "To be spiritually minded is life and peace" (Romans 8:6).[1]

In the New Testament, the encounter between God's Spirit and the human spirit is a fundamental aspect of the Christian experience (Galatians 6:18; Titus 3:5–6). It is "in the Spirit" that people encounter God and experience His life (Galatians 5:16–26). While the spirit remains an arena of struggle for believers, it is also the place in the human experience that we meet God personally. Different terms, such as *heart, spirit, soul,* and *mind,* refer to particular aspects of human existence, life, and consciousness.[2]

The term *spiritual* (Greek, *pneumatikos*) conveys the idea of belonging to the realm of the spirit. It is the inner life of human beings which embodies the nature and essence of the spirit. In the New Testament it is almost exclusively a Pauline word. Outside Paul's letters it occurs only in 1 Peter 2:5. Paul uses the word *spiritual* in three ways: (1) *adjective,* a spiritual something, e.g., "spiritual gifts"; (2) *masculine noun,* a "spiritual man"; (3) *neutral noun,* spiritual things or "things of the Spirit."[3]

Dallas Willard says that a spiritual life "consists in that range of activities in which people cooperatively interact with God—and with the spiritual order deriving from God's personality and action."[4] John Calvin, the great theologian, referred to the Holy Spirit as the "inward teacher" *(interior magister)* who speaks to our hearts. Calvin writes,

"But we must bring a ready teachableness; we must listen hard and pay attention if we want to progress in the school of God. Most of all, we need patience until the Spirit makes plain what we seemed to have often read or heard in vain."[5]

LIFE IN THE SPIRIT

The New Testament emphasizes that the true Christian life is a life in the Spirit (Ephesians 5:18). We are challenged to "walk in the Spirit" (Galatians 5:16), "be filled with the Spirit" (Ephesians 5:18), be "led by the Spirit" (Galatians 5:18); produce the "fruit of the Spirit (Galatians 5:22), "live in the Spirit" (Galatians 5:25), and exercise the "gifts" of the Spirit (Romans 12:6; 1 Corinthians 12:1). Biblical Christianity is a spiritual journey with Jesus Christ, led by the Spirit.

Over a century ago, the Scottish pastor Robert Candlish wrote, "For some, their life is not a walk with God, but a brief tumultuous rush of excitement, ending soon in vacancy, or something worse."[6] Whenever we fail to develop spiritually, our inner lives suffer. Instead of listening to God and walking with God, we almost lose all sense of God's presence in our lives. Our hearts become deadened, and God's voice in our soul is barely audible.

The greatest problem of postmodern society is its loss of transcendence. Without God, our lives tend to become a jumble of activities designed to deaden the pain of our hearts. Our inner beings cry out for God, but we silence the cry with our busy pursuit of material and personal gratification. Only in the end of the pursuit, do we finally ask ourselves, *What is still missing?*

Thomas Moore observed, "The greatest malady of the twentieth century [was] its loss of soul. When the soul is neglected, we experience obsessions, addictions, violence, loss of meaning and emotional pain."[7] No one has made a better assessment of the last century. As our society has become more complex and technological, it has also become more superficial. The emptiness of our times is revealed in a spiritual vacuum that cries out to be filled by the divine. We are no longer a predominantly Christian society. The heart and soul of the Western world has been polluted by the secular pursuit of life without God.

Charles Colson has referred to our national spiritual condition as the "New Dark Ages."[8] The barbarians of spiritual neglect are again threatening the soul of our society, and we may not be able to withstand the assault. Without a solid spiritual foundation, society quickly turns to selfism, relativism, and materialism. But such indulgence always leaves us empty and asking, "Isn't there anything more to life?" Ironically, excessive materialism almost always leads to mysticism. Society is never content without some belief in supernatural power.

Gary Collins writes, "Life is a spiritual journey. It is part of the human condition to be restless, aware that something or someone greater than we exists."[9] In light of this restless search, Collins observes a new spiritual awakening today unprecedented in modern times. "It is an unconventional and revolutionary movement," he suggests, "that is changing psychiatry, education, health care and thousands of churches."[10]

People are tired of psychological analysis, educational theory, and spiritual triviality. They want God! Nothing else. Nothing less. Their hurts cannot be satisfied with more electronic gadgets, impersonal technology, or new and improved commodities. Their hearts are crying out for a deep and personal relationship with God.

LONGING FOR GOD

Augustine called spirituality a "holy longing." Brent Curtis and John Eldredge call it a "sacred romance."[11] They write, "This longing is the most powerful part of any human personality. It fuels our search for meaning, for wholeness, for a sense of being truly alive. However we may describe this deep desire, it is the most important thing about us, our heart of hearts, the passion of our lives. And the voice that calls us in this place is none other than the voice of God."[12]

Humanity was created by God for fellowship with Him. We are never really fully satisfied without Him. Something deep within the human heart knows this to be true. In the depth of human agony and personal crisis, even the most irreligious will cry out, "Oh, God!" We know intuitively that He is there (see Romans 1:19–22). His voice is calling to us from every sunset, every waterfall, and every newborn baby. But all too often, His voice is silenced by the din of activity that causes us to focus on the creation, rather than the Creator.

God speaks, but we try to silence His voice with outward activity. We go for counseling, join a small group, read a book, or get religious. Curtis and Eldredge express it like this: "The voice in our heart dares to speak to us . . . Listen to me—there is something missing in all this . . . You were made for something more [and] you know it."[13] It is this "sacred romance," to know and love God with all our hearts, that calls to us deep within. It is more than God engaging our intellects. It is His passionate appeal to capture our hearts.

When God calls, we must respond. We must decide if this is His voice. If it is, we must believe that He is really God—that He is there after all, and that He cares about us individually and personally. Believing is the first step on the journey of faith that will ignite your soul, stretch your mind, and move your heart.

THE JOURNEY OF FAITH

Faith is so important that it is mentioned over three hundred times in the Bible The first reference to believing God is found in the story of Abraham. The scripture says: "[Abram] believed in the LORD, and He accounted it to him for righteousness" (Genesis 15:6). This particular step of faith was so important that it was quoted three times in the New Testament (Romans 4:3; Galatians 3:6; James 2:23).

The power of faith rests in the object of our faith. At the foundation of all love is a belief in the object that is loved. If I do not believe in a person, I cannot love him. The same is true in our relationship with God. Without faith it is impossible to know Him and love Him. Faith is the starting point in our spiritual journey. We must begin with God—believing that He exists, believing that He cares, and believing that His love is real.

The journey of faith is not a simple leap into the dark. It is far more than that. It begins with the assurance that God is really there. It moves ahead with great challenges—sometimes with moments of spiritual ecstasy and sometimes with long periods of spiritual drought. But ultimately the journey of faith is a spiritual pilgrimage that diminishes our confidence in earthly things and focuses our hopes on heaven. Every heartache, every disappointment with life, every human mistake and failure points us to someone beyond ourselves. Each struggle on the journey reminds us that we need God.

HEARTS ABLAZE

"Most Christians have lost the life of their heart, and with it, their romance with God," exclaim Curtis and Eldredge.[14] We started the journey well—excited with the discovery that God is truly on our side. But somewhere along the journey we became bogged down by the mundane. Consumed by the "tyranny of the urgent," we lost sight of our ultimate destination. When that happens in a believer's life, it robs him of the joy of the journey. In some cases, he almost forgets that he is on a spiritual journey.

God has several ways of calling us back. Sometimes He uses *silence*. After Abraham and Sarah put reason above revelation in the matter of having a child, God did not speak to them again for thirteen years (cf. Genesis 16:16; 17:1). When we haven't heard from God in a long time, we are more likely to listen when He does speak. Sometimes God speaks to us in *whispers*. Elijah was in deep depression, hiding in a cave, fearing for his life, when he heard the voice of God's "gentle whisper" (1 Kings 19:12 NIV). But other times, God *shouts* at us through our physical and emotional pain, our human failures, and our personal and financial crises. In our times of greatest need, we are more likely to hear His voice—correcting us, consoling us, and reminding us that we are His.

Feeling alone and isolated during a difficult time will break us of our self-sufficiency. It drives us to the only One who truly loves us. Jesus Himself faced this—His rejection, arrest, trial, and crucifixion would test the limits of His humanity. His disciples too would suffer isolation, persecution, and even death in His absence. But Jesus offered them the wonderful gift of His comfort. He promised to send the Holy Spirit as their Counselor (Greek, *parakleton*). He assured us that our own personal spiritual Counselor would keep our relationship with Christ vital and real every day.

Jesus' cross is the primary symbol of the Christian faith. It represents His substitution for our sins by which we can have a personal relationship with God. He died in our place in order to repair our relationship with God (2 Corinthians 5:18). The first step toward accepting that we can be made right with God is admitting that our relationship with Him has been damaged. Sin doesn't merely bruise that relationship, it completely severs it. Worse, it places us in an adversarial relationship with God that can cause us to spend a lifetime justifying ourselves instead of allowing Him to repair the relationship.

The broken relationship between us and God is not a superficial rift, and were it not for God's grace, it would entail a hopeless standoff. But God has taken the initiative to correct the problem. Jesus took our sin upon Himself and died so that it would no longer stand as an obstacle between us and God. Grace makes this provision possible and faith accepts it as a free gift.

The picture of Jesus knocking on the door in Revelation 3:20 is often represented as Him knocking on the door of the unbeliever's heart. But look carefully at the context (3:14–23). He is clearly knocking on the door of the church! They were in danger of locking the Lord of life outside the church. That's how we lose Him. We fill our churches and our Christian lives with everything but Him— until there's no room in our hearts.

True spirituality is centered in a personal relationship with Jesus Christ. Without Him, theology deteriorates into human philosophy. And without Him, spirituality becomes little more than a narcissistic quest for a mystical experience. But to really know Him is to know life as it was meant to be—a "sacred romance" with the lover of your heart and soul.

WHO IS JESUS CHRIST?

Prophets have a way of making people angry. They are blunt and sometimes tactless. They don't beat around the bush. They get right to the point.

And that's why they sometimes get themselves tossed behind bars.

Such was John the Baptist's fate. He told King Herod Antipas (Herod the Great's son) that he couldn't lawfully marry his brother's wife, Herodias. So Herod had him arrested and transported to the fortress at Machaerus, in the wilderness east of the Jordan River.

In jail, John began to ask himself deep and searching questions. Don't be surprised that he began to question his situation. He probably never expected to end up in jail, let alone face execution.

Death row! he may have thought. *I thought we were going to bring in the kingdom! I didn't mind giving up the spotlight—but I didn't mean to exit the stage altogether. We'd better get a few things straight here.*

John wasn't afraid to die; he simply wanted to make sure it was for the right cause. He heard Jesus was preaching in Galilee and attracting great crowds, so he sent messengers to reaffirm that He really was the Messiah (see Matthew 11:2–3).

You may think it a strange request, but when you are facing death, you will probably find yourself asking the same question. Is Jesus really who He said He is? Can I really trust Him with my eternal destiny? Honest questions from people facing life's greatest challenge: death.

Jesus was a prophet Himself, so His reply was to the point: "Go back and report to John what you hear and see: The blind receive sight, the lame walk, those who have leprosy are cured, the deaf hear, the dead are raised, and the good news is preached to the poor" (Matthew 11:4–5 NIV).

PROOF THAT HE WAS THE MESSIAH

Here was undeniable proof that He was the Messiah. Jesus gave sight to the blind. No one had ever done that. There is not one record in the Old Testament of a blind person receiving his sight. Not one!

He raised the dead. Only Elijah and Elisha had ever done that. He was operating on the highest levels of the miraculous. And His greatest miracles were yet to come— the resurrection of Lazarus and Himself!

The lame walked. The deaf heard. Lepers were cleansed. These are miracles performed only by God's greatest miracle-workers. And Jesus did them in abundance!

Yet He was more than a miracle-worker or a healer. He was a preacher of the gospel. "The good news is preached to the poor," he told John's disciples.

The Baptist understood what He meant. It was a fulfillment of Isaiah's prophecy. Isaiah 61:1 predicted of the Messiah, "The Spirit of the Lord GOD is upon me, because the LORD has anointed Me to preach good tidings to the poor."

Jesus' ministry fulfilled the Messianic prophecy in Isaiah 35:5–6: "Then the eyes of the blind shall be opened, and the ears of the deaf unstopped. Then the lame shall leap like a deer, and the tongue of the dumb sing."

Our Lord was reminding John the Baptist of all these prophecies he held so dear. Were they being fulfilled? Certainly they were, Jesus replied. It was a message of hope to His cousin, His forerunner, the one who had prepared the way for His ministry.

"[John] is Elijah who is to come," Jesus said (Matthew 11:14), referring to the prophecy of Malachi 4:5. He is the "messenger" sent ahead to prepare the way, an allusion to Malachi 3:1.

"There has not risen one greater than John the Baptist," Jesus proclaimed (Matthew 11:11). He was the greatest of the prophets. But even *he* wanted to be assured that Jesus was the One.

HIS MORAL SUPERIORITY

John found further confirmation in Jesus' superior moral integrity. Jesus towers above everyone in the gospel accounts. He is more kind, more wise, more gracious than anyone else. His love is abundant. His grace is exuberant. His mercy is endless. He is morally superior in every way.

"To what can I compare this generation?" Jesus asked. "They are like children sitting in the marketplaces," He explained (Matthew 11:16 NIV). They were like immature children, playing while their mothers shopped in the market. To pass the time, they would play their flutes to other children and expect them to respond accordingly. To them, life was a game.

Jesus said, "Wisdom is proved right by her actions" (Matthew 11:19 NIV). John the Baptist was a hermit, and people thought he had a demon. Jesus was a friend of sinners and they thought He had a demon as well.

You can't study Jesus' life and message and walk away unresponsive. His very nature demands that we make a choice. What's more, His call to discipleship demands that we make a choice. Either Christ or the world. Which will it be?

It's quite a choice! All or nothing. Jesus or the world. This life or the next. Time or eternity. His way or my way.

You too may be asking: Is He really the One? Or, do I look for someone else?

The disciples were faced with the same choice when multitudes began turning away from Him. "'You do not want to leave too, do you?' Jesus asked the Twelve. Simon Peter answered him, "Lord, to whom shall we go? You have the words of eternal life" (John 6:67–68 NIV).

If Jesus is not the answer, then who is? What other valid options do you have? Dead religions? Deceased leaders? Ritualistic structures? Legalistic regulations? Empty rituals? Mystical experiences?

No, the true and living Savior is the only viable answer. There is none like Him!

When at last we realize what we really want, we see that Jesus is all we really need.

LIAR, LUNATIC, OR LORD?

The Bible makes some bold claims about Jesus Christ. It presents Him as the Son of God, the Savior of the world, and the Lord of the universe. The New Testament even goes so far as to insist that our eternal salvation depends on our faith in Him.

You cannot read very far in the Gospels without asking yourself some serious questions:

Was Jesus who He claimed to be?

Is He really the only Savior?

Can I trust what He said?

Does it matter what I do with Him?

During the past two thousand years, millions of people have claimed Him as their Savior. They have staked their eternal destinies upon His promises. And they have ordered their lives according to His precepts.

If the story of Jesus is a lie, it is the greatest hoax ever perpetrated on the human race. But if it is the truth, then we must take Him seriously. To fail to do so could cost us everything.

Each of us must stop at some point and consider the question: Who is Jesus Christ? Was He a deceiver? Was He deceived? Or was He divine?

The Old Testament was written by numerous authors over a period of fifteen hundred years. Yet, from beginning to end, the Old Testament consistently and congruously predicted the coming of Christ. Consider just a few examples of these predictions:

Genesis 22:18	Born of the seed of Abraham
Genesis 49:10	Born of the tribe of Judah
Jeremiah 23:5	Born of the house of David
Isaiah 7:14	Born of a virgin
Micah 5:2	Born in the town of Bethlehem
Isaiah 9:7	Heir to the throne of David
Isaiah 53:3	Rejected by His own people
Psalm 41:9	Betrayed by a friend
Zechariah 11:12	Betrayed for thirty pieces of silver
Isaiah 53:12	Executed with criminals
Psalm 22:16	Pierced through the hands and feet
Zechariah 12:10	Crucified (see also Zechariah 13:6)
Isaiah 53:9	Buried with the rich
Isaiah 53:5	Atonement for all our sins
Psalm 16:10	Resurrected from the dead

It is highly unlikely that Jesus could have fulfilled all these prophecies by chance. It is also improbable that He deliberately tried to fulfill them. He had no human control over where and how He would be born, live, and die. All these fulfilled prophecies cannot be mere coincidence. Each one builds upon the others. Add them together and you have convincing proof that Jesus was the predicted Messiah.

Second, you cannot read the New Testament without concluding that Jesus claimed to be God. That claim brought charges of blasphemy, cries of anger, attempts at stoning, and finally, the crucifixion itself.

Why did the religious leaders demand that He be put to death? Because they understood the serious nature of His claims (NIV):

John 4:26	"I . . . am he" (the Messiah).
John 5:23	"He who does not honor the Son does not honor the Father."
John 5:39	"These are the Scriptures that testify about me."
John 6:40	"Everyone who looks to the Son and believes in him shall have eternal life, and I will raise him up at the last day."
John 8:58	"Before Abraham was born, I am!"
John 10:30	"I and the Father are one."
John 14:9	"Anyone who has seen me has seen the Father."

Jesus claimed to have come from heaven, to be equal with God, to be the very incarnation of God, and to represent the power and authority of God. There can be no doubt that He believed He was God.

And yet what a man *is* speaks louder than what he *does*. Look at the character of Jesus and you will see a man without sin, who is pure before all men. Even at His trial, His accusers found nothing with which to accuse Him. He never spoke an untrue word. He never made a promise He could not keep. His personal integrity was above reproach. He was fully human, yet truly divine.

There is no doubt that the people around Him believed He was God. Look at what they said about Him:

John the Baptist— "Look, the Lamb of God, who takes away the sin of the world!" (John 1:29 NIV)

John the apostle— "No one has ever seen God, but God the One and Only, who is at the Father's side, has made him known." (John 1:18 NIV)

Simon Peter— "You are the Christ, the son of the living God." (Matthew 16:16 NIV)

Nathanael— "Rabbi, you are the Son of God; you are the King of Israel." (John 1:49 NIV)

The Samaritans—	"[We] know that this is indeed the Christ, Savior of the world." (John 4:42)
The Jews—	"He was even calling God his own Father, making himself equal with God." (John 5:18 NIV)
The disciples—	"We . . . believe and know that You are the Christ, the Son of the living God." (John 6:69)
The disciples in the boat—	"Truly You are the Son of God." (Matthew 14:33)
Temple guards—	"No man ever spoke like this Man!" (John 7:46)
Martha—	"Yes, Lord, I believe that You are the Christ, the Son of God." (John 11:27)
Pontius Pilate—	"I find no fault in Him." (John 19:6)
Roman centurion –	"Truly this was the Son of God." (Matthew 27:54)
Doubting Thomas—	"My Lord and my God!" (John 20:28)

After you evaluate all the evidence for yourself, you too must ask: Who is Jesus Christ? Liar? Lunatic? Or Lord?

If He is a *liar* who deliberately deceived others, He is not worthy of your worship. If He is a *lunatic*, self-deceived, and out of touch with reality, He is not worthy of your devotion. But if He is indeed *Lord of lords,* then you have no choice but to bow down and worship Him as your Lord.

C. S. Lewis said, "A man who was merely a man and said the sort of things Jesus said would not be a great moral teacher. He would either be a lunatic—on the level with a man who says he is a poached egg—or else he would be the Devil of Hell. You must make your choice. Either this man was, and is, the Son of God: or else a madman or something worse. You can shut Him up for a fool, you can spit at Him and kill Him as a demon; or you can fall at His feet and call Him Lord and God."[15]

BELIEVING HIS PROMISES

Faith is believing. It is an act of trust by which we commit ourselves to someone or something. Jesus put it as simply as possible when He said, "Have faith in God" (Mark 11:22). Believe in God. Believe in His Person, His promises, and His power.

Faith is not optional. Either you believe or you don't. Either you trust God enough to love Him and entrust Him with your life, or you don't really believe Him and therefore can't love and trust Him.

Charles Spurgeon put it like this: "There lies at the bottom of all love a belief in the object loved, as to its loveliness, its merit or capacity to make us happy. If I do not believe in a person, I cannot love him. If I cannot trust God, I cannot love Him."[16]

Saving faith is reliant trust in Jesus Christ. It means that I believe He is who He claims to be and that He can do what He says He can do. I believe that He really loves me, that He wants to forgive me, and that His death on the cross is sufficient payment for my sins.

Trusting Jesus is more than believing He exists. It is more than believing that He lived a good life or that He died on a cross. It means believing that He is the Savior and that there is no greater Savior.

Faith in Christ means that I believe He died for *me.* That He rose again for *me.* That He is in heaven today interceding for *me.* And that He is coming again for *me.* Faith is my personal response to Jesus Christ. When I truly believe in Him, I am personalizing all that He has done for me, all that He offers to me, and all that He will continue to do on my behalf.

The Bible summarizes God's promise like this: "God has given us eternal life, and this life is in His Son. He who has the Son has life; he who does not have the Son of God does not have life" (1 John 5:11–12). This is about as personal as it gets.

Either you have Jesus or you don't. Either you have eternal life or you don't. Faith is the key that unlocks the door to heaven.

RECEIVING HIS GIFT

How does faith begin? By receiving. God has made us an offer. He has offered to forgive our sins. In fact, He has offered to exchange our sin for Christ's righteousness. Believing that offer to be sincere, we respond by receiving the gift God offers—the gift of eternal life!

We receive God's gift like a beggar reaches out for a piece of bread. We take it by faith. We claim it as our very own. When we receive Jesus Christ as our personal Savior, we receive all the benefits He offers: salvation, forgiveness, acceptance, righteousness, and eternal life.

Eventually, faith grows into confidence. Once we become convinced God's offer is for us, our faith grows into confidence in all of God's promises. We become more and more convinced that He really means what He has said. It begins with a simple act of reception and grows into confidence that results in a new lifestyle.

Saving faith should automatically grow into *living* faith. After all, if we can trust Jesus to take us to heaven, why wouldn't we trust Him to help us through the trials of the day? If His salvation is good enough for the future, why isn't it enough for today?

Faith results in obedience. As our confidence in God grows, it becomes easier to obey His will for our lives. Not only are we saved by faith, but we also grow into spiritual maturity by faith. We walk by faith. We live by faith.

The Bible explains living by faith in this way: "The life I live in the body, I live by faith in the Son of God, who loved me and gave himself for me" (Galatians 2:20 NIV). We learn to trust Him with our daily lives because we have trusted Him for our eternal destiny.

Once you step out by faith to take Jesus as your Savior, keep on walking by faith. In time, you will gain the confidence to run the race of life with Him. But you must begin by taking that first step! No more doubts. No more hesitations. No more excuses. It's time to believe Him. Step out by faith. Trust Him today.

15

Hope
for the Future

Do not let your hearts be troubled . . . I am
going there to prepare a place for you.
—JOHN 14:1–2 NIV

THE TIMING OF THE LAST DAYS IS IN GOD'S
hands. From a human standpoint it appears that we are
standing on the threshold of the final frontier. The pieces of
the puzzle are all in place. As the sands of time slip through
the hourglass of eternity, we are all moving closer to an
appointment with destiny. The only question is, How
much time is left?

The tension between living for today and looking for
tomorrow is one of the realities of the Christian life. We
often find ourselves caught between the here-and-now and

the hereafter. On the one hand, we need to be ready for Jesus to come at any moment. On the other hand, we have God-given responsibilities to fulfill in this world in the meantime.

We are living in a time of great crisis, but it is also a time of great opportunity. We must be prepared for the challenges that lie ahead of us:

- New technologies will make our lives more convenient, but they will also make us more dependent on those conveniences.

- Medical advancements will continue to pose enormous challenges in the area of biomedical ethics.

- The shifting sands of sociopolitical change will also challenge our national and international policies in the days ahead.

All told, we will find ourselves living in a very different world from the one into which we were born. All of these changes and challenges will confront us in the days ahead.

Preparing for Christ's return is something each one of us must do for ourselves. No one else can get our hearts ready to meet God. You and I must do that ourselves. Jesus urges us to do three things in view of His second coming:

1. Keep watching (Matthew 24:42).

2. Be ready (Matthew 24:44).

3. Keep serving (Matthew 24:46).

Erwin Lutzer, the senior pastor of Moody Church in Chicago, has reminded us that there are "five unshakable pillars" to enable us to withstand the onslaught of secularism in our society today:[1]

1. God still reigns.

Human leaders will come and go. Some will be better, some worse. Some will be what we deserve—a reflection of our own weakness and sinfulness. But behind the scene of human governments, God still reigns over the eternal destiny of mankind. Beyond this temporal world, God rules from the throne in heaven. He guides His children and overrules in the affairs of men and nations to accomplish His will and purposes. The Bible assures us "there is no authority except from God" (Romans 13:1). Regardless of who our leaders are, we are to offer "prayers, intercession and thanksgiving . . . for kings and those in authority (1 Timothy 2:1–2 NIV).

2. The church is still precious.

During this present age, God is still working through His church to evangelize the world. Jesus gave us clear direction about what we are to be doing until He returns. He said, "Go and make disciples of all nations, baptizing them in the name of the Father and of the Son and of the Holy Spirit, and teaching them to obey everything I have commanded you . . . to the very end of the age" (Matthew 28:19–20 NIV). The church may flourish or be persecuted in the days ahead, but she is to be faithful to her mission until Jesus calls her home to glory (1 Thessalonians 4:13–17).

3. Our mission is still clear.

The church stands as the salt and light of God in society. We are to "proclaim the praises of Him who called you out of darkness into His marvelous light" (1 Peter 2:9). Lutzer suggests that we can accomplish this by, (1) representing Christ to the world by a godly lifestyle; (2) winning people to Christ through intellectual and moral confrontation with a loving persuasiveness; and (3) strengthening our families as a testimony to God's grace. The integrity of sincere and authentic Christian lives and families speaks volumes to a lost world that is desperate for meaning and purpose. We cannot underestimate the spiritual impact that true Christianity has on those who have no answers to the overwhelming problems of life. Bill Hybels has said, "When Christians live out their faith with authenticity and boldness . . . they create quite a stir just being themselves."[2]

4. Our focus is still heaven.

It is easy for modern American Christians to forget that heaven is our real destiny. So many believers today live in such peace and affluence that they forget about heaven. We actually think that God's purpose is to bless our lives here on earth. Dave Hunt has observed, "Unfortunately, too many persons—even dedicated Christians—find heaven a topic of only minor interest because they consider it irrelevant to the challenges of this present life."[3] We must remember, however, that this world is no friend to grace. As time passes, we should expect a continual moral decline in secular society. The Bible reminds us that there will be an "increase of wickedness" and that "terrible times" will come in the last days (Matthew 24:12; 2 Timothy 3:1 NIV). In the meantime, whatever success we have in this world must be measured in the light of our eternal destiny. Joe Stowell reminds us that if we make heaven our primary point of reference it will transform our relationship to everything that is temporal in this world.[4] C. S. Lewis wrote, "Christians who did most for the present world were just those who thought most of the next."[5]

5. Our victory is still certain.

The ultimate Bible prophecies focus on the triumph of Christ and His bride—the church (Revelation 19).

They assure us that we will share in His victorious reign. Whatever transpires in the meantime must be viewed in light of our eternal destiny. Peter Marshall, former chaplain of the U.S. Senate, said, "It is better to fail at a cause that will ultimately succeed than to succeed in a cause that will ultimately fail."[6] Until the trumpet sounds and the Lord calls us home, we have the Great Commission to fulfill and the world to evangelize. There is no reason to let up now. Since we have no clear date for the termination of the present age, we must keep on serving Christ until He comes.

A young African martyr wrote these words in his prison cell before he died:

"I'm part of the fellowship of the unashamed, the die has been cast, I have stepped over the line, the decision has been made—I'm a disciple of Jesus Christ—I won't look back, let up, slow down, back away or be still.

"My past is redeemed, my present makes sense, my future is secure—I'm finished and done with low living, sight walking, smooth knees, colorless dreams, tame visions, worldly talking, cheap giving and dwarfed goals.

"My face is set, my gait is fast, my goal is heaven, my road is narrow, my way is rough, my companions are few, my guide is reliable, my mission is clear. I won't give up, shut up, let up until I have stayed up, stored up, prayed up for the cause of Jesus Christ.

"I must go till He comes, give till I drop, preach till everyone knows, work till He stops me and when He comes for His own, He will have no trouble recognizing me because my banner will have been clear."[7]

WHAT SHOULD WE BE DOING?

Since we can never be sure when God's purposes for His church will be finalized, we must remain obedient to our Lord's commands regarding His church. This was made clear to the disciples at the time of Christ's ascension to heaven. They had asked if He was going to restore the kingdom to Israel at that time, and Jesus told them, "It is not for you to know the times or seasons which the Father has put in His own authority" (Acts 1:7). Two facts are clear in this statement: (1) The date has been set; and (2) we aren't supposed to know it because we have a responsibility to fulfill in the meantime.

In the very next verse, Jesus gave the Great Commission, telling the disciples they would be empowered by the Holy Spirit to be His witnesses in Jerusalem, Judea, Samaria, and "to the end of the earth" (Acts 1:8). Then, to their amazement, He ascended into heaven, leaving them gazing intently into the sky. Two men in white (probably angels) appeared and asked, "Why do you stand here looking into the sky? This same Jesus, who has been taken from you into heaven, will come back in the same way you have seen him go into heaven" (Acts 1:11).

All too often, today's Christians are just like those early disciples. We spend more time gazing into the sky and speculating about Christ's return than we do serving Him. The angels' point was to remind the disciples that His return is certain. Thus we shouldn't waste time and energy worrying about when or whether Christ will return. Believe that He is coming again on schedule and be about His business in the meantime.

Jesus left several instructions about what we ought to be doing while we await His coming:

1. Witness for Him everywhere you go. Our Lord told His disciples to be His witnesses everywhere—even to the farthest ends of the earth (Acts 1:8).

2. "Go into all the world and preach the gospel" (Mark 16:15). This command emphasizes the evangelistic and missionary nature of the church's ministry during the present era. We are to take the gospel to the whole world.

3. "Repentance and forgiveness of sins will be preached in [my] name to all nations" our Lord declared in Luke 24:47 NIV. Calling men and women to repent and believe the gospel is the twofold nature of the evangelistic enterprise.

4. "Make disciples of all the nations, baptizing them," Jesus said in Matthew 28:19. Making converts and discipling them in their walk with God is a major emphasis of the church's mission.

5. Build the church, in every generation. Jesus told His disciples that He would build His church with such power that "the gates of hell shall not prevail against it" (Matthew 16:18 KJV). Jesus pictured the church being on the march until He calls her home.

6. "Work . . . until I come back" (Luke 19:13), Jesus said in the parable of the talents. In this parable, the servants were to "put this money to work" until their master returned. We are to stay busy about the Master's business until He returns.

7. Remain faithful until He returns. Our Lord concluded His prophetic message in the Olivet Discourse by reminding His disciples to continue in faithful and wise service even though He might be gone a long time (Matthew 24:45; 25:14–21).

IS THERE ANY HOPE FOR OUR GENERATION?

With God, there is always hope. Always.

For the church our greatest hope is a revival of the heart, a revival in all that matters in our relationships with God. In fact, genuine spiritual revival is the result of the outpouring of the Holy Spirit on the church. Throughout history, God often has moved to bless His people in a fresh and powerful way. Genuine revival came as God's people were convicted of their sin, repented, and gained a new zeal and devotion for God in their lives.

In revival, the self-centered, halfhearted indifference that so often dominates our lives is swept aside by a new and genuine desire to live for God.

Revival begins to renew our values and redirect our lives. It calls us to a more serious walk with Christ and results in substantial and abiding fruit (see John 15:16; Galatians 5:22–23). The changes that occur, both in individual believers and in the church collectively, speak convincingly to the world about what it really means to belong to Christ. Such revival comes when God's people pray, when God's truth is proclaimed, and when God's Spirit moves in our lives.

Unfortunately, there is little evidence of genuine revival today; some have lost hope of it altogether. Others have diluted the gospel message in order to make its appeal more acceptable to today's generation. Evangelist Bailey Smith has correctly observed, "The Christ of the Bible has been reduced to a fallible humanitarian. Salvation has been repackaged into a feel-good experience. Forgotten in today's 'gospel revisionism' is the message that sent Christ to the cross and the disciples to martyrdom. Today's gospel 'lite' is hardly worth living for and certainly not worth dying for."[8]

If we are going to make an impact on our generation for the cause of Christ, it must be soon. Since we have no idea how much time is left, we dare not let the time slip away indiscriminately. If we are going to use wisely whatever time God gives us, we must be about His business with a sense of urgency. On the one hand, we dare not *presume* on God's grace by assuming we have plenty of time left to get the job done. On the other hand, we dare not *terminate* the grace of God by assuming it is too late for our generation.

Prophecy lovers are especially prone to this second re-action. We are eschatological pessimists. We know all too well that things are going to get worse, not better. We believe that a growing religious apostasy is strangling the spiritual life out of our churches. And we have little hope in human efforts to revitalize our dying culture. Therefore, it is easy for us to give up and quit trying to reach our generation with the gospel.

This is the downside to the pretribulational position. It *can* (not must) lead to a kind of eschatological "fatalism." If we are not careful, we can abandon our calling and just sit and wait for the rapture. But there is no biblical warrant for such fatalism. The Bible never tells us that things will be so bad that we should give up and quit preaching altogether and wait for "the end." Rather, the Bible clearly instructs us to keep preaching, testifying and witnessing, knowing that Christ will continue to build His church until He comes (Matthew 16:18).

In the meantime, we can live with our eyes on the skies—watching for Christ to come—and with our feet on the earth, working for Him until He comes. This balance of *expectation* (that Jesus could come at any moment) and *participation* (serving Him faithfully until He comes) is what the Christian life is really all about. Living in the light of His coming keeps us focused on what is really important in life. It also keeps our attention on the balance between our present responsibilities and our future expectations.

God has moved supernaturally throughout the centuries. It would be just like the Lord of grace to move again in "seasons of refreshing" with one great ingathering of souls just before the rapture of the church. He calls us to be His witnesses in this world. Let us pray for one last great revival before He calls us home.

The hope of the second coming is the strongest encouragement for us to live right until Jesus comes. The ultimate incentive to right living is the fact that we will face our Lord when He returns. Each of us needs to be ready when that day comes. If we faithfully live out whatever time is left, we will surely hear Him say, "Well done, good and faithful servant! You have given Me all your heart!"

Epilogue:
Happy Endings

TONIGHT MICAH PHILLIPS'S CRISIS INTERVENTION meeting would be different.

The same people were there—broken and despondent as ever. The businessman who had lost his family, the woman who had swindled her company, the waitress who had been raped by a stranger. But there was a new feeling in the air— and a few new faces in the crowd. Mark Adams's wife, Susan, was there. So was Rick, Rhonda Willagher's husband.

"I asked you all to come tonight because I have something important to tell you," Micah began. "It's not easy for someone like me to admit this. We counselors like to be the ones who help everyone else. Maybe it's our way of avoiding our own problems."

All eyes were focused on Micah as she spoke. There was something different in her tone of voice, and everyone present knew it. She seemed like a different person. Even her body language spoke of honesty and brokenness.

"I've always thought of myself as a caring person," Micah continued, "but the last time we met, I had come to the end of myself. My own problems were so overwhelming that I just couldn't respond to you properly."

She went on to explain her own story to them, her fear, her despair, and her indifference to their problems when they last met. Then she asked them to forgive her for failing them that in that previous meeting.

"We're all human," Rhonda offered. "We understand what you're going through."

"Isn't that why we're all here?" asked Mark, sympathetically. "We just want to know that somebody cares."

"Well, there is something else I need to tell you," Micah added. "I've known for years that something was missing in my life. I tried to push it aside. We call that 'sublimation' in psychology. I thought that if I cared enough about others, that would make up for it. I—"

"You seem different," the waitress interrupted.

"I am," Micah replied. "I've met someone who has totally changed my life."

Micah watched as her clients glanced knowingly at one another and smiled winsomely.

"No, not that," Micah inserted, laughing. "When we last met, I left here emotionally exhausted. But the next morning I met someone who told me what was missing in my life. As he talked with me, I knew he was right. What was missing was God. I had been running from Him for years.

"Ever since I was a teenager, I've tried to fill my life with helping others because I wouldn't accept the help He was offering me." Micah went on to explain the decision she had made to receive Jesus Christ as her personal Savior.

"I stopped trying to fix myself and decided to give myself to Him," Micah continued. "I learned what it really means to be forgiven—and to be willing to forgive. That's what I want to share with you tonight. Each of us needs forgiveness, and there's only one person who can give us both forgiveness and eternal comfort for the problems we face: That's God. He is the One who changed me. And I know He can do the same for each of you."

Everyone listened intently as Micah explained the love of God to them and shared how they, too, could know God's forgiveness and begin a relationship with Him.

Though not all were enthusiastic about their counselor's message, none could deny a presence, a special glow in their circle. God was there and they all knew it.

They still had a long way to go, but for the first time they were headed in the right direction.

Notes

Chapter One

[1] Silvan Tomkins, *Affect, Imagery and Consciousness* (New York: Springer, 1993), 26ff.

[2] Dan Allender, "Emotions and the Pathway to God," *Christian Counseling Today* (Winter 1996): 33.

[3] Ibid., 35. This is basically the same point taken by Tim LaHaye in his various books on temperament theory. See *Why You Act the Way You Do* (Wheaton, Ill.: Tyndale House, 1988).

4 Larry Crabb, "Struggling Without a Shepherd," *Christian Counseling Today* (Spring 1995): 15.

5 Colin Brown, ed., *The New International Dictionary of the New Testament*, vol. 2, (Grand Rapids, Mich.: Zondervan, 1981), 180–184.

6 A. C. Meyers, ed., *Eerdmans Dictionary of the Bible* (Grand Rapids, Mich.: Eerdmans, 1987), 471.

7 Walter Elwell, ed., *Baker Encyclopedia of the Bible*, vol. 1 (Grand Rapids, Mich.: Baker, 1988), 939.

8 Ibid., 939.

9 William Holladay, *A Concise Hebrew and Aramaic Lexicon of the Old Testament* (Grand Rapids, Mich.: Eerdmans, 1971), 172. The pief form of *lebab*, "intelligent," can be rendered to "take away" or "bewitch" the heart (cf. Song of Solomon 4:9). Holladay lists ten meanings for "heart" (Hebrew, *leb*): (1) physical organ, (2) seat of vitality, (3) inner self, (4) mind and character, (5) determination, (6) intention, (7) understanding, (8) the self, (9) conscience, (10) inner life (171–172).

10 Robert Boyd Munger, *My Heart—Christ's Home* (Chicago: InterVarsity Press, 1964).

11 Ibid., 6.

12 Ibid., 19.

13 Quoted in Roy Aldrich, *Walking with the Lord* (Detroit: Detroit Bible College, 1961), 2.

14 Ibid.

15 W. G. T. Shedd, *Dogmatic Theology*, vol. 7 (Nashville: Thomas Nelson, 1983), 188.

Chapter Two

1 Gary Collins, *The Soul Search* (Nashville: Thomas Nelson, 1998), 23.
2 Ibid.
3 Ibid., 24.
4 D. James Kennedy, *The Gates of Hell Shall Not Prevail* (Nashville: Thomas Nelson, 1996), 89.
5 Don Wildmon, "It Is Time to End Religious Bigotry," *American Family Association Journal* (July 1995), 21.
6 Based on Joanne Harris's novel, *Chocolat* (New York: Penguin Books, 1999).

Chapter Three

1 Quoted by Lawrence White at Concerned Women for America Conference, Washington, D.C., 1995.
2 Thomas Moore, *Care of the Soul* (New York: Harper Collins, 1992), xi.
3 Brent Curtis and John Eldredge, *The Sacred Romance* (Nashville: Thomas Nelson, 1997), 4.
4 Larry Crabb, *Finding God* (Grand Rapids, Mich.: Zondervan, 1993), 46.
5 Ibid., 40.
6 This concept is developed at length in Tim LaHaye and

David Noebel, *Mind Siege: The Battle for Truth in the New Millennium* (Nashville: Word, 2000), 103–212.

[7] Cf. Martin Anderson, *Imposters in the Temple* (New York: Simon & Schuster, 1992); Alan Bloom, *The Closing of the American Mind* (New York: Simon & Schuster, 1986); Ronald Nash, *The Closing of the American Heart* (Dallas: Probe Books, 1990); David Nobel, *Understanding the Times* (Eugene, Oreg.: Harvest House, 1991); and Ed Dobson and Ed Hindson, *The Seduction of Power* (Old Tappan, N.J.: Revell, 1988).

Chapter Four

[1] Jean Kilbourne, *Deadly Persuasion* (New York: Free Press, 1999).

[2] Robert Sylvester, "The Effects of Electronic Media on a Developing Brain," in *Media Literacy Online Project,* College of Education, University of Oregon. Cf. also, "How Emotions Affect Learning," in *Educational Leadership* (October 1994), 20–28.

[3] Ibid.

[4] Ibid.

[5] George Gerbner, quoted by Kilbourne, *Deadly Persuasion,* 27.

[6] Marshall McLuhan, quoted by Kilbourne, *Deadly Persuasion,* 31.

7 Learned Hand, quoted in Robert Fitzhenry, *The Fitzhenry & Whiteside Book of Quotations* (Toronto: Fitzhenry & Whiteside Limited, 1993), 19.

8 Malcolm Muggeridge, quoted in Eric Clark, The *Want Makers* (New York: Penguin Books, 1988), 371.

9 Eric Fromm, *To Have or To Be?* (New York: Harper & Row, 1976), 110.

10 "Five Core Concepts About Media," from the Center for Media Literacy (Los Angeles). On the Web at http:uoregon.edu/coreconcepts.htm

11 "National Television Violence Study" by the Center for Communication and Social Policy at the University of California, Santa Barbara (2001). On the Web at http://research.ucsb.edu.ccsp

12 Arlene Moscovitch, *Electronic Media and the Family* (Toronto: Vanier Institute of the Family, 1998), 1.

13 Stephen Kline, *Out of the Garden: Toys and Children's Culture in an Age of TV Marketing* (London: Verso, 1993), 29. See also "Video Game Culture: Leisure and Play Preferences of B. C. Teens," Simon Fraser University, British Columbia, Canada (1998).

14 Survey reported in *The Ottawa Citizen* (April 13, 1998).

15 Moscovitch, *Electronic Media*, 3.

16 John Pungente, Jesuit Communications Project, Toronto, Canada. Quoted by Moscovitch, n. *Electronic Media*, 56.

17 Moscovitch, *Electronic Media,* n. 56.

18 George Gerbner, quoted by Moscovitch, *Electronic Media,* 6.

19 "Joint Statement on the Impact of Entertainment Violence on Children," at Congressional Public Health Summit (July 26, 2000). Signed by Donald Cook, president, American Academy of Pediatrics; Michael Honaker, deputy chief executive officer, American Psychological Association; Clarice Kestenbaum, president, American Academy of Child & Adolescent Psychiatry; Ratcliffe Anderson, Jr., executive vice president, American Medical Association.

20 Ibid.

21 Ibid.

22 Franklin Zimring, quoted by John Cloud, "The Legacy of Columbine," *Time* (March 14, 2001), 15.

23 David Grossman, transcript from *60 Minutes* telecast (April 25, 1999).

24 Debbie Pelley, quoted in *Time* (March 14, 2001), 13.

25 Robert Sylvester, op.cit., p. 11.

Chapter Five

1 Quoted by Charles Colson, *Against the Night* (Ann Arbor, Mich.: Servant, 1989), 55.

2 Ibid., 133–34.

3 2 Thessalonians 2:3.

4 See Ed Hindson, *Is the Antichrist Alive and Well?* (Eugene, Oreg.: Harvest House, 1998).

5 Barbara Marx Hubbard, *The Book of Co-Creation: An Evolutionary Interpretation of the New Testament,* unpublished manuscript dated 1980. Quoted by Lalonde, *One World,* 166–67.

6 Michael Horton, ed., *The Agony of Deceit* (Chicago: Moody Press, 1990).

7 Marvin Stone, "What Kind of People Are We?" *U. S. News & World Report* (February 5, 1979).

8 Francis Schaeffer and C. Everett Koop, M.D., *Whatever Happened to the Human Race?* (Old Tappan, N.Y.: Revell, 1979), 89.

Chapter Six

1 A. T. Pierson, *The Bible and Spiritual Life* (Fincastle, Va.: Scripture Truth, reprint of 1887 Exeter Hall lectures), 169.

2 C. S. Lewis, *Mere Christianity* (New York: MacMillan, 1960), 53–54.

3 E.g., see Martin Anderson, *Imposters in the Temple* (New York: Simon & Schuster, 1992).

4 Hank Hanegraaff, *Christianity in Crisis* (Eugene, Oreg.: Harvest House, 1993).

5 "Children of the Apocalypse," *Newsweek* (May 3, 1993): 30.

6 Allan Bloom, *The Closing of the American Mind* (New York: Simon & Schuster, 1986), 25–85.

7 Ibid., 34.

8 Ibid., 82–85.

9 Harold Bussell, *Unholy Devotion: Why Cults Lure Christians* (Grand Rapids, Mich.: Zondervan, 1983), 61–72.

10 David Breese, *The Marks of a Cult* (Eugene, Oreg.: Harvest House, 1998).

11 Ibid., 51.

12 Christopher Edwards, *Crazy for God* (Englewood Cliffs, N.J.: Prentice-Hall, 1979), 200.

13 Elliot Miller, *A Crash Course in the New Age Movement* (Grand Rapids: Baker, 1989), 17–18.

Chapter Seven

1 Paul Johnson, *Modern Times: The World from the Twenties to the Eighties* (San Francisco: Harper & Row, 1983). A perceptive treatment of current trends by the eminent British historian.

2 See the development of this theme in Francis Schaeffer, *How Should We Then Live?* (Old Tappan, N.J.: Revell, 1976), 130–66.

3 This issue is discussed by a variety of evangelical writers. See R. C. Sproul, *Lifeviews*, 113–27; Richard Neuhaus, *The Naked Public Square*, 94–143; Carl

F. H. Henry, *Christian Countermoves in a Decadent Culture* (Portland: Multnomah Press, 1986), 31–46; Francis Schaeffer, *The Great Evangelical Disaster* (Westchester, Ill.: Crossway Books, 1984), 111–46.

4 For a brilliant assessment of this method of thinking and its influence on religion, see Harry Blamires, *The Christian Mind* (Ann Arbor, Mich.: Servant Books, 1978), 3–66.

5 Allan Bloom, *The Closing of the American Mind* (New York: Simon & Schuster, 1987). The underlying theme is that higher education has failed democracy and impoverished the souls of today's students.

6 Ibid., 19.

7 Ibid., 25–43.

8 Ibid., 82.

9 Ibid., 85.

10 Arthur Levine, *When Dreams and Heroes Died: A Portrait of Today's College Student* (San Francisco: Jossey-Bass Publishers, 1980). In this study sponsored by the Carnegie Foundation for the Advancement of Teaching, Levine observes that today's students are self-centered, individualistic escapists who want little responsibility for solving society's problems, but who want society to provide them with the opportunity to fulfill their desires.

11 This point is argued strongly by Francis Schaeffer in *The Great Evangelical Disaster*, 141–51. In fact,

Schaeffer insists that the disaster among evangelicals is their accomodation to the spirit of the age, which will lead to "the removal of the last barrier against the breakdown of our culture."

12 Francis Schaeffer and C. Everett Koop, *Whatever Happened to the Human Race?* (Old Tappan, N.J.: Revell, 1979).

13 Peter Singer, "Sanctity of Life or Quality of Life," *Pediatrics* (July 1983), 128–129.

14 Cal Thomas, "Taking the Hypocritical Oath," in *Occupied Territory* (Nashville: Wolgemuth & Hyatt, 1987), 22–24.

15 Stuart Briscoe, *Playing by the Rules* (Old Tappan, N.J.: Revell, 1986), 98–99.

16 Quoted by Tim LaHaye, *The Race for the 21st Century* (Nashville: Thomas Nelson, 1986), 135.

17 Ibid., 139–42.

18 Sproul, *Lifeviews.*

19 Ibid., 69.

20 Francis Schaeffer, *A Christian Manifesto* (Westchester, Ill.: Crossway Books, 1981).

21 For a history of this conflict, see Ed Dobson, Ed Hindson, and Jerry Falwell, *The Fundamentalist Phenomenon* (Garden City, N.Y.: Doubleday, 1981), 47–77.

22 Francis Schaeffer, *Escape from Reason* (Chicago:

InterVarsity Press, 1968). This concept is discussed throughout Schaeffer's first book and is presented in a limited diagram on page 43.

[23] Ibid., 43–44.

[24] See Richard J. Newhaus, "Religion: From Privilege to Penalty," *Religion & Society Report* (March 1988): 1–2.

[25] Charles Colson, *Kingdoms in Conflict* (Grand Rapids: Mich.: Zondervan, 1989), 220–23.

[26] Ibid., 221.

[27] Ibid., 221. He quotes James Wall in the *Christian Century* without a specific reference.

[28] Ibid., 222.

[29] Sproul, *Lifeviews*, 35.

[30] See T. J. Altizer and W. Hamilton, *Radical Theology and the Death of God* (New York: Bobbs-Merrill, 1966). For an evangelical response, see John W. Montgomery, *The "Is God Dead?" Controversy* (Grand Rapids: Zondervan, 1966).

[31] Sproul, *Lifeviews*, 37.

[32] Truman Dollar, "The Drift Away from Life," *Fundamentalist Journal* (March 1988): 58.

[33] Os Guinness, *The Dust of Death* (Downers Grove, Ill.: InterVarsity Press, 1973), 17ff.

[34] Ibid., 17.

[35] Ibid., 25.

[36] Ibid., 25–26, quoting Jean-Paul Sartre, *Nausea*

(Baltimore: Penguin Books, 1965), 191.

[37] Guinness, ibid., 28–29.

[38] Zhores Medvedev, *A Question of Madness* (New York: Alfred Knopf, 1971). See also "Psychoadaptation, or How to Handle Dissenters," *Time* (September 27, 1971), 45.

[39] Guinness, *Dust of Death*, 28–29.

[40] For a general survey of New Age teachings, see the Spiritual Counterfeits Project study by Karen Hoyt, *The New Age Rage* (Old Tappan, N.J.: Revell, 1987).

[41] Ibid., 21–32.

[42] See William Kilpatrick, *The Emperor's New Clothes: The Naked Truth About the New Psychology* (Westchester, Ill.: Crossway Books, 1985); and Garth Wood, *The Myth of Neurosis* (New York: Harper & Row, 1986).

Chapter Eight

[1] Elliot Miller, *A Crash Course on the New Age Movement* (Grand Rapids: Baker, 1989), 24.

[2] Ibid., 21–22.

[3] Marilyn Ferguson, *The Aquarian Conspiracy* (Los Angeles: J. P. Tarcher, 1980). Her claims may be overstated, but they certainly represent the hopes and dreams of New Age evangelists.

[4] Constance Cumbey, *The Hidden Dangers of the Rainbow* (Shreveport, La.: Huntington House, 1983);

Miller, *Crash Course,* 107.

5 Mark Satin, *New Age Politics* (New York: Dell Books, 1978).

6 Joe Klimo, *Channeling* (Los Angeles: J. P. Tarcher, 1987), 185.

7 Sanaya Roman and Duane Packer, *Opening to Channel* (Tiburon, Calif.: H. J. Kramer, 1987), 127.

8 C. S. Lewis, *Screwtape Letters* (London: Collins, 1964), 25.

9 Shakti Gawain, *Creative Visualization* (San Rafael, Calif.: New World Library, 1978), 15.

10 Ibid., 18.

11 Ibid., 36–40.

12 Miller, *Crash Course*, 15.

13 Ibid., 16.

14 Fritjof Capra, *The Turning Point* (Toronto: Bantam Books, 1982), 302.

15 Miller, *Crash Course,* 65.

16 Donald Keys, *Earth at Omega: Passage to Planetization* (Boston: Branden Press, 1982), iv.

17 John White, "Channeling: A Short History of a Long Tradition," *Holistic Life* (Summer 1985): 20.

18 Cumbey, *Hidden Dangers,* 7.

Chapter Thirteen

1 Quoted in Tim LaHaye, *Spirit-Controlled Temperament* (Wheaton, Ill.: Tyndale House, 1992), 97.

² Ibid., 98.

³ Ibid., 103.

Chapter Thirteen

¹ Bruce Demarest, *Satisfy Your Soul* (Colorado Springs: Nav Press, 1999), 92.

² Ibid., 94.

³ Ibid., 98.

⁴ Leon Morris, *Testaments of Love* (Grand Rapids, Mich.: Eerdmans, 1981), 276.

⁵ Ibid.

⁶ J. I. Packer, *Keep in Step with the Spirit* (London: Hodder & Stoughton, 1991), 74–75; Cf. also his *A Quest for Godliness: The Puritan Vision of the Christian Life* (Westchester, Ill.: Crossway Books, 1990).

⁷ Demarest, *Satisfy Your Soul,* 120.

⁸ Ibid.

⁹ See Tim LaHaye, *Power of the Cross* (Sisters, Oreg.: Multnomah Books, 1996).

¹⁰ C. S. Lewis, quoted in Ed Hindson and Ed Dobson, eds. *Knowing Jesus Study Bible* (Grand Rapids, Mich.: Zondervan, 1999), 1579.

Chapter Fourteen

¹ Quoted in Gary Collins, *The Soul Search* (Nashville: Thomas Nelson, 1998), 1

2 "Spirit," in *Eerdmans Bible Dictionary* (Grand Rapids, Mich.: Eerdmans, 1987), 967.

3 "Spirit/Spiritual," in Colin Brown, ed., *New International Dictionary of New Testament Theology,* vol. 3 (Grand Rapids, Mich.: Zondervan, 1971), 706–707.

4 Dallas Willard, *The Spirit of the Disciplines* (San Francisco: Harper Collins, 1988), 18.

5 John Calvin, *The Gospel According to St. John* (Grand Rapids: Eerdmans, 1960 edition), 88.

6 Robert Candlish, *A Commentary on 1 John* (Edinburgh: Banner of Truth, reprint of 1870 edition), 105.

7 Thomas Moore, *Care of the Soul* (New York: Harper Collins, 1992), xi.

8 Charles Colson, *Against the Night* (Ann Arbor, Mich.: Servant Publications, 1989), 55.

9 Gary Collins, *The Soul Search* (Nashville: Thomas Nelson, 1998), 1.

10 Ibid., 5.

11 Ibid., 11.

12 Brent Curtis and John Eldredge, *The Sacred Romance* (Nashville: Thomas Nelson, 1997), 7.

13 Ibid., 2.

14 Ibid., 10.

15 C. S. Lewis, *Mere Christianity* (New York: Macmillan, 1960), 56.

16 Charles H. Spurgeon, quoted by Calvin Linton,

"Faith," in Carl Henry, ed., *Basic Christian Doctrines* (New York: Holt, Rinehart and Winston, 1962), 203.

Chapter Fifteen

1. Erwin Lutzer, *Where Do We Go from Here?* (Chicago: Moody Press, 1993), 25–48.
2. Bill Hybels, *Becoming a Contagious Christian* (Grand Rapids, Mich.: Zondervan, 1994), 43, 59.
3. Dave Hunt, *Whatever Happened to Heaven?* (Eugene, Oreg.: Harvest House, 1988), 7.
4. Joseph Stowell, "Set Your Mind on Heaven," in *10 Reasons Why Jesus Is Coming Soon* (Sisters, Oreg.: Multnomah Books, 1998), 235ff.
5. C. S. Lewis, *Mere Christianity* (New York: Macmillan, 1943), 118.
6. Quoted by Lutzer, *Where Do We Go?* 46.
7. Ibid., 47.
8. Bailey Smith, *Taking Back the Gospel* (Eugene, Oreg.: Harvest House, 1999), 8.

Acknowledgments

OUR GRATEFUL ACKNOWLEDGMENTS TO KAREN Kingsbury for her expert editorial assistance and guidance during the development of this book, and to Emily Boothe, who so graciously typed the original manuscript. Their work and patience are greatly appreciated.